D1360906

TASTES OF THE SEA

BRIMAR

Photography: Nathalie Dumouchel
Selection, adaptation and development of recipes: Josée Robitaille
Food stylist: Josée Robitaille
Prop stylist: Isabelle Beaudin
Tableware courtesy of: Arthur Quentin
                                 Geneviève Lethu
                                 La Maison d'Émilie
                                 Pier 1 Imports
                                 Stokes

Cookware courtesy of: Regal Ware Inc.

The publisher wishes to thank the following for their collaboration:
Poissonnerie la Reine de la Mer (Paul Talbot and his team), and RAMCA Tile Inc.

Graphic design: Zapp
Typesetting: Typotech Inc.

Copyright © 1998 Brimar Publishing Inc.
338 St. Antoine St. East
Montreal, Canada H2Y 1A3
Telephone: (514) 954-1441
Fax: (514) 954-5086

All rights reserved. No part of this publication may be reproduced, stored in a retrieval system, or transmitted in any form or by any means, electronic, mechanical, photocopying, recording, or otherwise, without the prior written permission of Brimar Publishing Inc.

The information in this book is true and complete to the best of our knowledge. All recommendations are made without any guarantees on the part of the author and the publisher. They disclaim all liability in connection with the use of this information.

ISBN 2-89433-303-X
Printed in the U.S.A.

CONTENTS

INTRODUCTION 4

GUIDE FOR SUBSTITUTING FISH 5

COOKING METHODS FOR FISH 6

PREPARATION TECHNIQUES 7

FINE HERBS 14

SPICES 15

SALADS 16

SOUPS 32

RAW, MARINATED, SMOKED 54

DEEP-FRIED 74

STEAMED 98

POACHED 118

SAUTÉED 142

BRAISED 176

IN THE OVEN 196

GRILLED 224

SAUCES 250

INDEX 254

INTRODUCTION

Fish and seafood are remarkable foods. They are very nutritious, easy to prepare, and versatile. As this book will show you, they can be cooked in many different ways and served with a wide variety of accompaniments.

Thanks to state of the art conservation techniques and to the speed of transportation, your local fish store can now offer a wide range of fish and seafood from around the world.

Rich in proteins and vitamins, fish has tender flesh that is low in calories and easy to digest. Fish is also an excellent source of phosphorous, magnesium, iron and iodine. It can be divided into three categories, according to its fat content:

- lean fish has less than 5% fat (sole, skate, porgy, etc.);
- medium-lean fish has between 5% and 10% fat (sardines, salmon, etc.);
- oily fish has more than 10% fat (tuna, mackerel, eel, etc.).

As for seafood, it can be divided into two groups:

- crustaceans (lobster, crab, shrimp, etc.)
- mollusks (oysters, mussels, scallops, etc.).

All are low in fat and are excellent sources of protein and mineral salts.

Buying Fish and Seafood

Whether you're buying fish or seafood, certain indicators of quality can help you make the right choices. Look for the following characteristics to ensure that you are buying the best quality.

Whole fresh fish: moist, red gills; bright, bulging eyes; shiny skin that sticks to the flesh; firm, elastic flesh; a pleasant, subtle odor.

Cut fresh fish: firm, elastic, bright flesh; pleasant odor.

Smoked fish: flesh that is a rich color and is not dried out; pleasant odor.

Frozen fish: firm, shiny flesh, with no signs of freezer-burn, snow or ice crystals; airtight packaging.

Canned fish: a can that has no bulges or dents.

Live crustaceans: heavy and lively; clean shells without green or black stains; bright eyes; firm flesh; pleasant odor.

Frozen crustaceans: no snow or ice crystals; moist flesh; airtight packaging.

Mollusks: alive until cooked; shell intact; pleasant odor; when you knock an open shell it should shut tight; if it doesn't, it should be discarded.

Fresh octopus, squid and cuttlefish: firm flesh with a thick, sticky coating.

Conservation

Fresh fish should be eaten as soon as possible after it is bought. A whole fish will keep longer if it has been cleaned and gutted, because it is the enzymes in its stomach that accelerate the process of deterioration. To keep fish in the refrigerator, it is best to wrap it in plastic wrap and cover it with ice. However, if it has already been cut into steaks or fillets, it should not be placed directly on ice, as it would lose some of its color and juice. Crustaceans and mollusks will keep a few days in the refrigerator; octopus, squid and cuttlefish should be kept on ice.

Freezing

Household freezers freeze food more slowly than commercial ones, which can cause the formation of ice crystals. This can affect both the texture and the flavor of fish. It is therefore best to set your freezer to its lowest possible temperature, so that the fish freezes as quickly as possible and doesn't lose any of its juice or texture in the process.

GUIDE FOR SUBSTITUTING FISH

~

Atlantic Salmon	*Pacific Salmon, Salmon Trout*
Black Sea Bass	*Striped Bass, Sea Bass, Red Snapper*
Bluefish	*Bonito, Sea Trout, Pike*
Bonito	*Mackerel, Tuna*
Carp	*Pike, Cod*
Cod	*Haddock, Halibut, Hake, Pike*
Eel	*Conger Eel*
Grouper	*Black Sea Bass, Striped Bass, Gray Mullet*
Gurnard	*Sea Bream, Scorpion Fish, Porgy*
Haddock	*Hake, Plaice, Sole, Turbot*
Halibut	*Cod, Grouper, Turbot*
Herring	*Mackerel, Sprat*
John Dory	*Sole*
Mackerel	*Swordfish, Herring, Tuna*
Monkfish	*Cod, Halibut, Grouper*
Pacific Salmon	*Atlantic Salmon, Salmon Trout*
Pike	*Cod, Whitefish*
Plaice	*Sole, Flounder*
Pompano	*Butterfish, Scabbardfish, Sole*
Porgy	*Sea bream, Scabbardfish*
Rainbow Trout	*Salmon, Salmon Trout*
Red Mullet	*Sea Bream, Gray Mullet, Gurnard*
Red Bream	*Sea Bream, Gilt-Head Bream*
Red Snapper	*Sea Bream, Red Bream, Red Mullet*
Salmon Trout	*Salmon, Rainbow Trout, Char*
Sardine	*Anchovy, Smelt, Small Mackerel*
Sea Bass	*Black Sea Bass, Striped Bass, Red Snapper*
Sea Bream	*Red Mullet, Porgy, Grouper*
Shark	*Swordfish, Sea Bass, Tuna*
Skate	*None*
Smelt	*Anchovy, Small Mackerel, Sardine*
Sole	*Plaice, Pike, Flounder*
Striped Bass	*Black Sea Bass, Sea Bass, Red Snapper*
Swordfish	*Bonito, Sea Bass, Tuna*
Tilefish	*Cod, Striped Bass, Sea Bass*
Sea Trout	*Bluefish, Cod, Haddock*
Tuna	*Bonito, Swordfish*
Turbot	*Cod, Haddock, Plaice, Pompano*

This guide suggests substitutions for fish that might not be readily available, or alternatives to vary the recipe. The substitutions are not necessarily exact equivalents for the fish type called for in the recipe.

Cooking Methods for Fish

FISH	smoked	raw[1]	marinated	steamed	poached	braised	fried	sautéed	baked	grilled
Black Sea Bass		●		●	●	●		●	●	●
Bluefish					●	●	●	●	●	●
Bonito		●		●	●	●		●	●	●
Carp				●	●		●	●	●	
Cod				●	●	●	●	●	●	
Eel	●			●	●			●	●	
Grouper		●				●	●	●	●	●
Gurnard				●	●			●	●	
Haddock	●		●	●	●	●		●	●	
Halibut				●	●	●		●	●	●
Herring			●				●	●	●	●
John Dory				●	●	●		●	●	
Mackerel	●		●				●	●	●	●
Monkfish				●	●	●		●	●	
Pike				●	●		●	●	●	
Plaice	●	●		●	●	●		●	●	
Pompano	●					●		●	●	
Porgy				●	●		●			●
Rainbow Trout	●			●	●			●	●	●
Red Bream		●	●	●				●	●	●
Red Mullet					●		●	●	●	●
Red Snapper	●	●		●	●		●	●	●	●
Salmon[2]	●	●	●	●	●		●	●	●	●
Salmon Trout	●			●	●					
Sardine			●				●	●	●	
Sea Bass	●	●	●	●	●	●		●		
Sea Bream		●	●	●				●	●	●
Shark					●	●	●	●	●	
Skate					●	●		●	●	
Smelt							●	●	●	●
Sole		●		●	●		●	●	●	
Striped Bass		●		●	●	●		●	●	
Swordfish	●	●	●			●	●	●	●	●
Tilefish				●		●			●	
Sea Trout	●			●	●			●	●	●
Tuna		●	●				●	●	●	●
Turbot		●		●	●		●	●	●	●

[1] Obviously, 'raw' is not a cooking method.
However it is worth pointing out which kinds of fish can be prepared
as sushi, sashimi, etc.

[2] Atlantic and Pacific salmon.

CLEANING FISH

1. *With kitchen scissors, cut off the dorsal fin.*

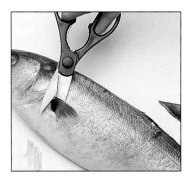

2. *Then cut off the other fins.*

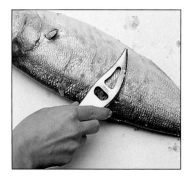

3. *With a scaler, scale the fish from the tail up to the head.*

4. *Or use the blunt side of a knife to scale the fish.*

5. *Using the point of a knife, cut down the underside of the fish.*

6. *Remove the entrails.*

7. *Wash the inside and outside of the fish thoroughly under cold, running water.*

BONING FISH

1. Hold the cleaned fish open and run the blade of a sharp knife between the flesh and the ribs to detach them.

2. With the point of a knife, cut along the backbone on both sides, from the tail towards the head.

3. Cut through the backbone at the base of the head, then pull it up from the head towards the tail. Cut through the other end at the base of the tail.

FILLETING FISH

1. Without cutting off the head, cut through the gills of the fish.

2. With the blade of the knife, cut along the backbone from just behind the head to the tail, cutting as close as possible to the bone.

3. Lift the fillet away, sliding the knife between the flesh and the ribs.

4. Turn the fish over and lift away the other fillet.

5. Slide the blade between the flesh and the ribs and remove the ribs.

6. Remove any remaining small bones with tweezers.

SLICING FILLETS
~

Slice the fillet into 1½ inch (3.5 cm) wide pieces.

SLICING ESCALOPES
~

With a sharp knife, cut wide pieces by placing the knife slightly on the diagonal.

CUTTING OUT STEAKS
~

Use a round fish that has been cleaned. Cut the head, then carve out 1-inch (2.5 cm) thick slices.

PREPARING TOURNEDOS
~

1. *Remove the backbone from the steak.*

2. *Remove about 1 inch (2.5 cm) of flesh from the ends.*

3. *Fold the loose skin around the flesh.*

4. *Tie the steak with string.*

SKINNING A FLAT FISH

1. *Cut through the skin just above the tail of the fish.*

2. *Lift the skin with the point of the knife.*

3. *Holding the fish firmly by the tail with a cloth, peel the skin away from the cut towards the head. Turn the fish over and repeat.*

BONING SARDINES

1. *Cut off the head.*

2. *With a knife, cut along the underside, remove the entrails and wash the cavity.*

3. *Slide the knife blade between the flesh and the ribs, on each side.*

4. *With the point of the knife, detach the backbone on both sides, up to the tail.*

5. *Pull on the backbone all the way to the tail and, if necessary, cut the end with scissors.*

SHELLING OYSTERS

1. *Wash oysters thoroughly under cold running water.*

2. *Insert the point of the oyster knife into the hinge, at the narrow end of the oyster. Twist the knife slightly to open the shell.*

3. *Hold the oyster firmly with a cloth and slide the blade along the inside from one end to the other.*

4. *With the knife, cut through the connecting muscle to detach the oyster from its shell.*

PREPARING SHRIMP

1. *Peel off the shell with your fingers.*

2. *Cut down the back of the shrimp.*

3. *Remove the vein.*

CLEANING MUSSELS

~

Scrub well and debeard mussels
by pulling on the byssus
protruding from the shell, then
wash under cold water.

PREPARING SQUID

~

1. Detach the head and
tentacles from the body by
holding the tentacles and
pulling gently.

2. Remove the transparent
cartilage inside the body, called
the "quill", and any remaining
entrails.

3. Remove the fins.

4. Peel off the skin and wash
the body of the squid.

5. Remove the beak and
discard.

6. Cut eyes from tentacles and
discard.

Preparing Lobster

1. *Break the tail section away from the body.*

2. *Break the tail open and remove the meat.*

3. *Detach the legs by breaking them at the joint.*

4. *Separate each claw from the rest of the leg.*

5. *Detach the small part of each claw.*

6. *With lobster pincers or a nut cracker, break open the claws and remove the meat.*

FINE HERBS

~

OREGANO

BAY LEAVES

THAI BASIL

MINT

ROSEMARY

THYME

CORIANDER

CHIVES

SAGE

CHERVIL

PARSLEY

BASIL

DILL

TARRAGON

SORREL

GARLIC CHIVES

SPICES

~

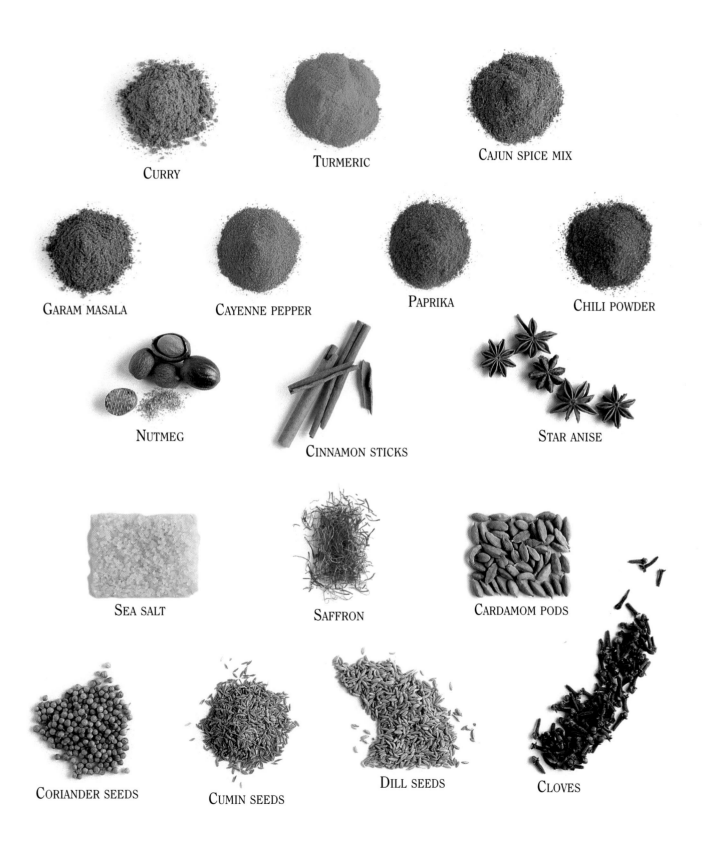

CURRY

TURMERIC

CAJUN SPICE MIX

GARAM MASALA

CAYENNE PEPPER

PAPRIKA

CHILI POWDER

NUTMEG

CINNAMON STICKS

STAR ANISE

SEA SALT

SAFFRON

CARDAMOM PODS

CORIANDER SEEDS

CUMIN SEEDS

DILL SEEDS

CLOVES

SALADS

~

Salads make for succulent entrées and delicious main dishes alike, any time of year. Whether served hot or cold, with a tangy or creamy vinaigrette, they are always nutritious and refreshing.

In this chapter, you'll discover a selection of tempting salad ideas where vegetables and greens combine with fish and seafood to whet the appetite and please the palate.

SHRIMP SALAD WITH GARLIC CROSTINI ≈

2	garlic bulbs	2
3 tbsp	extra virgin olive oil	45 mL
20	medium shrimp, peeled and deveined	20
2	dry shallots, chopped	2
4 tbsp	mayonnaise (see p. 250)	60 mL
2 tbsp	chili sauce*	30 mL
8	slices French bread, crusts trimmed, cut in 3	8
½	bunch rapini, washed and dried	½
½	red bell pepper, finely diced	½
½	yellow bell pepper, finely diced	½
8	cherry tomatoes, halved	8
	juice of ½ lemon	
	salt and freshly ground pepper	

Brush garlic bulbs with olive oil.

≈ Preheat oven to 400°F (200°C). Brush garlic bulbs with 1 tbsp (15 mL) olive oil. Wrap bulbs in aluminum foil and cook 30 minutes in oven.

≈ Meanwhile, bring a large pot of water to a boil, add shrimp and cook about 4 minutes; rinse in cold water, drain and set aside. In a large bowl, combine shallots, mayonnaise and chili sauce; season to taste. Add shrimp, mix well and set aside.

≈ To prepare the crostini, brush pieces of bread with olive oil and toast under broiler in oven. Set aside.

≈ Sprinkle rapini with lemon juice, season and distribute among 4 salad plates. Top with shrimp mixture and garnish with diced bell peppers and cherry tomatoes.

≈ When garlic bulbs are cool enough to handle, peel and place 1 clove on each crostini. Serve with the salad.

Wrap bulbs in aluminum foil.

Peel the grilled garlic.

4 SERVINGS

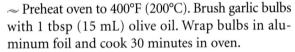

*NOTE: CHILI SAUCE IS A VERY HOT MIXTURE OF CHILI PEPPERS, VINEGAR AND SALT. A MILDER, SWEET CHILI SAUCE IS ALSO AVAILABLE.

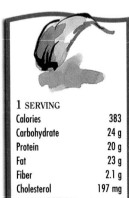

1 SERVING	
Calories	383
Carbohydrate	24 g
Protein	20 g
Fat	23 g
Fiber	2.1 g
Cholesterol	197 mg

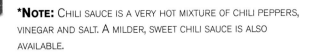

SALMON TROUT SALAD WITH WALNUT OIL VINAIGRETTE ~

½ cup	dry white wine	125 mL
1 cup	water	250 mL
4	salmon trout fillets, unskinned	4
1 tbsp	balsamic vinegar	15 mL
1 tbsp	walnut oil	15 mL
2 tbsp	peanut oil	30 mL
1 tbsp	chopped fresh chervil	15 mL
½ lb	mesclun*	225 g
1	lemon, peeled and sliced	1
	juice of ½ lemon	
	salt and freshly ground pepper	

~ Place wine, water and lemon juice in a large sauté pan. Bring to a boil and cook 4 minutes over medium heat. Reduce heat to low and add fillets; cook 4 minutes.

~ Meanwhile, prepare the vinaigrette: combine balsamic vinegar, walnut oil, peanut oil and chervil; season to taste.

~ Drain fish and cut each fillet in half; place two pieces on each plate. Serve with mesclun. Sprinkle with vinaigrette and garnish with lemon slices.

4 SERVINGS

*NOTE: MESCLUN, ORIGINALLY FROM THE SOUTH OF FRANCE, IS A MIXTURE OF DIFFERENT SALAD GREENS AND YOUNG SHOOTS SUCH AS LAMB'S LETTUCE, ENDIVE, RADICCHIO AND ROCKET LETTUCE. THE NAME IS DERIVED FROM THE NIÇOIS WORD 'MESCLUMO', MEANING MIXTURE.

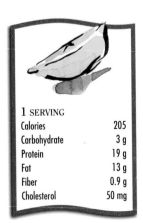

1 SERVING	
Calories	205
Carbohydrate	3 g
Protein	19 g
Fat	13 g
Fiber	0.9 g
Cholesterol	50 mg

~~~~~~~~~~~~~~~~

*NOTE: FISH SAUCE, OR 'NAM PLA', IS A THIN BROWN SAUCE MADE FROM SALTED AND FERMENTED ANCHOVIES. IT IS WIDELY USED IN SOUTHEAST ASIA AND IS A STAPLE INGREDIENT IN THAI COOKING.

SPICY SQUID SALAD, THAI STYLE

6	fresh squid	6
2 tbsp	peanut oil	30 mL
½	red bell pepper, finely chopped	½
½	red chili pepper, seeded and finely chopped	½
1	garlic clove, finely chopped	1
2 cups	bok choy, chopped	500 mL
1 tbsp	fish sauce (nam pla)*	15 mL
4 tbsp	coconut cream	60 mL
2 tbsp	chopped fresh coriander	30 mL
2 tbsp	chopped fresh garlic chives	30 mL
	juice of ½ lime	
	sea salt	

~ Clean squid thoroughly (as shown on page 12) and slice into ¼ inch (0.5 cm) rings. In a large saucepan, heat oil over high heat. Add squid, season with salt and sauté 2 minutes.

~ Reduce heat to medium. Add bell pepper, chili pepper, garlic and bok choy. Cook 2 minutes. Add fish sauce, lime juice and coconut cream; mix well. Sprinkle with coriander and chives. Serve warm.

4 SERVINGS

1 SERVING	
Calories	291
Carbohydrate	13 g
Protein	26 g
Fat	15 g
Fiber	1.1 g
Cholesterol	350 mg

MARINATED HERRING AND BEET SALAD

⅔ lb	marinated herring	300 g
2	new potatoes, unpeeled	2
3 tbsp	sunflower oil	45 mL
1	small onion, finely chopped	1
1 tbsp	white wine vinegar	15 mL
2	medium beets*, cooked and sliced	
	fresh dill for garnish	
	salt and freshly ground pepper	

∼ Drain herring well, slice and set aside. Cook potatoes in salted boiling water, about 20 minutes. Remove from water and let cool.

∼ Meanwhile, prepare vinaigrette: combine sunflower oil, onion and wine vinegar. Season to taste, mix well and set aside.

∼ Slice the potatoes. Divide herring, beets and potatoes among 4 salad plates and top with vinaigrette. Garnish with fresh dill and serve.

4 SERVINGS

*NOTE: IT IS BEST TO COOK BEETS BEFORE PEELING THEM. THE SKIN IS THEN EASILY REMOVED BY PRESSING DOWN ON THE VEGETABLE WITH YOUR FINGERS.

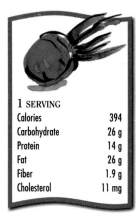

1 SERVING	
Calories	394
Carbohydrate	26 g
Protein	14 g
Fat	26 g
Fiber	1.9 g
Cholesterol	11 mg

*NOTE: AN OPENED FRESH OYSTER SHELL SHOULD SHUT WHEN YOU KNOCK ON IT. IF IT DOESN'T, THE OYSTER IS DEAD AND IT SHOULD BE DISCARDED.

THE DAIKON RADISH IS A JAPANESE VARIETY OF RADISH THAT IS MILDER THAN OTHER TYPES.

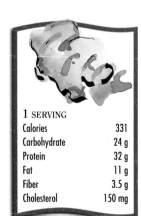

1 SERVING	
Calories	331
Carbohydrate	24 g
Protein	32 g
Fat	11 g
Fiber	3.5 g
Cholesterol	150 mg

FRESH OYSTER AND SPINACH SALAD

10 oz	fresh spinach	300 g
24	oysters	24
2 tbsp	soy sauce	30 mL
1 tbsp	mirin (Japanese rice wine)	15 mL
1 tbsp	rice vinegar	15 mL
½ tsp	chopped fresh ginger	2 mL
1 tbsp	sunflower oil	15 mL
2	carrots, cut in julienne	2
1 cup	thinly sliced fresh daikon radish*	250 mL
	freshly ground pepper	

~ Wash spinach, drain and set aside in a bowl.

~ Wash oysters and remove from shells, reserving liquid.

~ To prepare the vinaigrette, mix together oyster liquid, soy sauce, mirin, rice vinegar, ginger and sunflower oil.

~ Season spinach with pepper and sprinkle with vinaigrette; mix well. Place spinach in the center of each plate, and the oysters around it; sprinkle with vinaigrette.

~ Top spinach salad with daikon and carrot julienne, and serve.

4 SERVINGS

MEXICAN ESCABÈCHE WITH ORANGE

1 lb	haddock or turbot fillets, sliced	450 g
1 tbsp	olive oil	15 mL
4 tbsp	extra virgin olive oil	60 mL
2	bay leaves	2
2	dry shallots, finely chopped	2
1	garlic clove, finely chopped	1
1 tbsp	chopped fresh chives	15 mL
1 tbsp	chopped fresh coriander	15 mL
	juice of 1 orange	
	zest of ½ orange	
	juice of 1 lemon	
	salt and freshly ground pepper	
	orange slices for garnish	

≈ Season slices of haddock with salt and pepper. In a sauté pan, heat 1 tbsp (15 mL) olive oil over high heat. Fry the haddock about 30 seconds on each side; set aside.

≈ In a large glass or ceramic dish, mix together extra virgin olive oil, orange juice and zest, lemon juice, bay leaves, shallots and garlic. Add the fish and marinate for 1 hour, carefully turning slices over after 30 minutes.

≈ Add chives and coriander; garnish with orange slices. Serve with corn chips, if desired.

4 SERVINGS

*NOTE: ESCABÈCHE IS A TECHNIQUE ORIGINALLY FROM SPAIN WHEREBY FISH IS FRIED OR LIGHTLY BROWNED, THEN MARINATED FOR 24 HOURS IN A SPICY, COOKED MARINADE. THE FISH WILL THEN KEEP FOR UP TO A WEEK IN THE REFRIGERATOR.

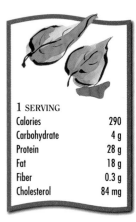

1 SERVING	
Calories	290
Carbohydrate	4 g
Protein	28 g
Fat	18 g
Fiber	0.3 g
Cholesterol	84 mg

POACHED SALMON AND ASPARAGUS SALAD

6 cups	water	1.5 L
1	carrot, peeled and sliced	1
1	leek, white part only, sliced	1
1	onion, sliced	1
1	fresh thyme sprig	1
2	fresh parsley sprigs	2
2	salmon steaks	2
2 cups	cooked, diced potatoes	500 mL
⅓ cup	mayonnaise (see recipe p. 250)	75 mL
1 tbsp	chopped fresh tarragon	15 mL
16	small asparagus shoots, cooked and cut into pieces	16
	fresh tarragon sprigs for garnish	
	salt and freshly ground pepper	

≈ Pour water into a large saucepan and add carrot, leek, onion, thyme and parsley; bring to a boil. Reduce heat to medium-low. Add salmon steaks and cook 7 to 8 minutes.

≈ Meanwhile, mix together potatoes, mayonnaise and tarragon; season well. Divide among 4 plates, and arrange asparagus around potatoes.

≈ Once salmon is cooked, remove from saucepan; discard skin and bones. Break salmon into chunks and place over potato salad. Garnish with tarragon sprigs and serve.

4 SERVINGS

≈≈≈≈≈≈≈≈≈≈≈≈≈≈≈≈≈≈≈

*NOTE: ADD SALMON BONES TO STOCK IN SAUCEPAN AND CONTINUE COOKING, ABOUT 20 MINUTES. PASS THROUGH A SIEVE AND USE THE STOCK FOR SOUPS OR OTHER RECIPES. STOCK CAN BE FROZEN FOR UP TO 3 MONTHS.

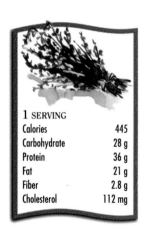

1 SERVING	
Calories	445
Carbohydrate	28 g
Protein	36 g
Fat	21 g
Fiber	2.8 g
Cholesterol	112 mg

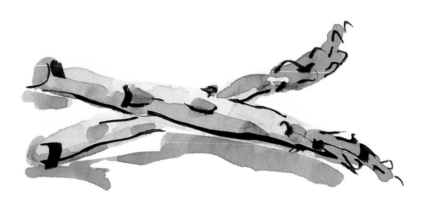

WARM HADDOCK SALAD WITH BELL PEPPERS ~

1 tbsp	rice vinegar	15 mL
1 tbsp	sesame oil	15 mL
3 tbsp	peanut oil	45 mL
¾ lb	haddock fillets*, in 4 pieces	350 g
½ each	green, red, yellow and orange bell pepper, thinly sliced	½
	juice of ½ lemon	
	juice of ½ lime	
	daikon radish shoots	
	mixed greens	
	salt and freshly ground pepper	
	white and black sesame seeds	

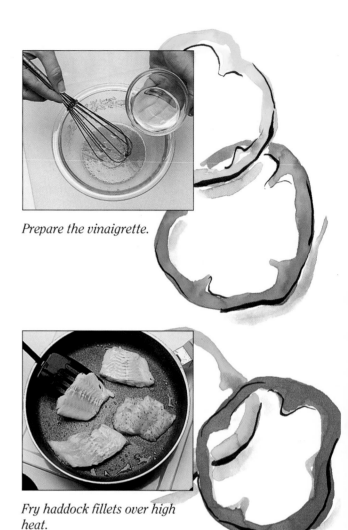

Prepare the vinaigrette.

~ To prepare the vinaigrette, combine rice vinegar, lemon and lime juice, sesame oil and 2 tbsp (30 mL) peanut oil. Set aside.

~ Heat a saucepan over high heat. Add remaining peanut oil. Season haddock fillets well and fry 5 minutes on each side. Remove from heat and add vinaigrette and bell peppers.

~ Place one piece of haddock on each plate, along with peppers, daikon shoots and greens. Sprinkle with vinaigrette and garnish with sesame seeds. Serve immediately.

4 SERVINGS

~~~~~~~~~~~~~~~~~~~~~~~~~~~~~~~

***NOTE:** YOU CAN USE HAKE OR FRESH COD INSTEAD OF HADDOCK.*

Fry haddock fillets over high heat.

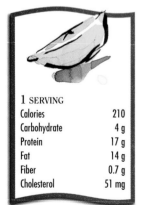

1 SERVING	
Calories	210
Carbohydrate	4 g
Protein	17 g
Fat	14 g
Fiber	0.7 g
Cholesterol	51 mg

Add peppers and vinaigrette.

OCTOPUS SALAD WITH KALAMATA OLIVES

2 lbs	baby octopus	1 kg
1½ cups	red wine	375 mL
1	garlic clove, crushed	1
1	onion, chopped	1
2	fresh oregano sprigs	2
4 tbsp	extra virgin olive oil	60 mL
1 cup	Kalamata olives*, pitted and quartered	250 mL
2 tbsp	red wine vinegar	30 mL
2 tbsp	chopped fresh parsley	30 mL
1 tbsp	chopped fresh oregano	15 mL
	salt and freshly ground pepper	

≈ Hold the octopus firmly by the head. With a sharp knife, cut through flesh below the eyes, separating the head from the tentacles. Discard the head. Clean the tentacles under cold, running water and tenderize with a mallet. Tentacles should feel soft but not rubbery.

≈ Plunge octopus into a pot of boiling water and cook for 5 minutes. Drain well and let stand until cool. Cut into 1 inch (2.5 cm) pieces. Place pieces in a pot and add red wine, garlic, onion and oregano sprigs.

≈ Cover and bring to a boil. Reduce heat to low and let simmer 45 minutes or until tender. Add olive oil, olives, wine vinegar, parsley and chopped oregano. Season to taste with salt and pepper. Let cool and serve.

4 SERVINGS

*NOTE: KALAMATA OLIVES (FROM GREECE) ARE BLACK OLIVES TREATED WITH A MIXTURE OF BRINE, OLIVE OIL AND WINE VINEGAR.

1 SERVING	
Calories	365
Carbohydrate	9 g
Protein	35 g
Fat	21 g
Fiber	2.2 g
Cholesterol	108 mg

~~~~~~~~~~~~~

*NOTE: OIL FLAVORED WITH BASIL IS A SEASONING OIL; IT IS NOT RECOMMENDED FOR COOKING. IT ENHANCES THE FLAVOR OF SALADS AND OTHER FOODS SUCH AS PIZZA, PASTA AND GRILLED FISH.

LOBSTER AND SCALLOP SALAD WITH BASIL OIL ~

1 tbsp	olive oil	15 mL
12	scallops	12
2 tbsp	balsamic vinegar	30 mL
4 tbsp	basil oil* (see recipe p. 252)	60 mL
1	head leaf lettuce, sliced	1
1	bunch dandelion leaves	1
½	fennel bulb, cut lengthwise into 4	½
2	lobster tails, cooked and cut into rounds	2
	salt and freshly ground pepper	

~ Heat olive oil in a sauté pan over high heat. Add scallops, season and cook 1 minute on each side; remove from heat. Combine balsamic vinegar and basil oil and pour over scallops; set aside.

~ Wash and dry lettuce and dandelion leaves, and divide among 4 plates. Add one slice of fennel to each and season with salt and pepper. Top with lobster and scallops. Drizzle with vinaigrette and serve immediately.

4 SERVINGS

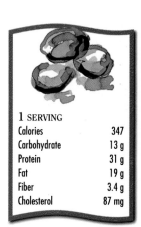

1 SERVING	
Calories	347
Carbohydrate	13 g
Protein	31 g
Fat	19 g
Fiber	3.4 g
Cholesterol	87 mg

SOUPS

~

Served at the beginning of a meal, a savory soup

tantalizes the taste buds and sets the tone for what will

follow. But certain soups are so hearty and delicious

that they can be served as meals in themselves!

The rich aroma of a soup simmering on the stove is

a welcome invitation to one and all. And when fish

and seafood are part of the temptation, who can

resist? Easy to prepare, the following recipes are

sure to please everyone, even the cook!

SEAFOOD AND SAFFRON SOUP

6 cups	fish stock	1.5 L
4	potatoes, peeled and cubed	4
1 cup	pearl onions	250 mL
1	large pinch saffron*	1
8	fresh clams, washed and scrubbed	8
12	mussels, washed, scrubbed and bearded	12
1½ lbs	tilefish, cubed	675 g
12	medium scallops	12
1	red bell pepper, diced	1
4 tbsp	chopped fresh parsley	60 mL
	salt and freshly ground pepper	

∾ Place 5 cups (1.25 L) fish stock in a large saucepan. Add potatoes and onions, and bring to a boil. Reduce heat to medium, cover and cook 10 minutes.

∾ Meanwhile, brown saffron* 1 minute in a small skillet over high heat. Add to potatoes.

∾ Place remaining fish stock, clams and mussels in another saucepan. Cover and cook over high heat until shells open. Discard any unopened shells. Set clams, mussels and cooking liquid aside.

∾ Add tilefish and scallops to the potatoes and onions and cook 5 minutes. Add reserved clams, mussels and liquid. Add red pepper and parsley; correct seasoning and simmer 5 minutes.

6 SERVINGS

*NOTE: TO GET THE MOST FLAVOR OUT OF SAFFRON, INFUSE IT FIRST IN A HOT LIQUID. NEVER FRY IT IN VERY HOT FAT.

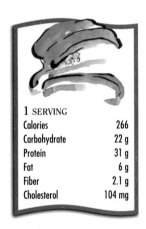

1 SERVING	
Calories	266
Carbohydrate	22 g
Protein	31 g
Fat	6 g
Fiber	2.1 g
Cholesterol	104 mg

SHRIMP WONTON SOUP

1	chicken carcass	1
1 lb	beef or veal bones	450 g
4 tbsp	dried shrimp	60 mL
1	onion, chopped	1
2	carrots, thinly sliced	2
1 lb	fresh medium shrimp	450 g
2	eggs	2
1 tbsp	dry sherry	15 mL
40	wonton* wrappers	40
2 cups	sliced choy-sum or spinach	500 mL
	chopped green onions	
	soy sauce	
	salt and freshly ground pepper	

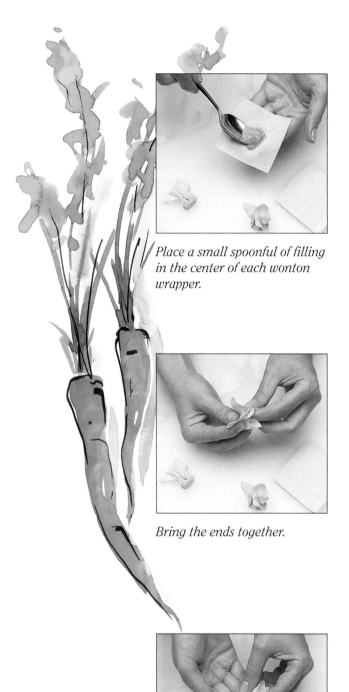

Place a small spoonful of filling in the center of each wonton wrapper.

Bring the ends together.

Turn over and press down on the filling to seal the wonton.

~ Rinse carcass and bones thoroughly under running water and place in a stewpot. Add dried shrimp, onion and carrots. Cover with water and bring to a boil; skim as needed. Reduce heat to low and let simmer 1½ hours, adding water if necessary. Pass the bouillon through a sieve and pour it back into the pot; set aside.

~ Meanwhile prepare the filling: peel fresh shrimp and purée in a blender. Add eggs, one at a time, and then sherry. Season with salt and pepper.

~ Place a small spoonful of filling in the center of each wonton wrapper and bring the ends together. Turn over and press down on the filling to seal the wonton.

~ Plunge the wontons in boiling salted water, 10 at a time, for about 5 minutes. Drain and add them to the bouillon. Add choy-sum and cook 3 minutes over high heat. Garnish with chopped green onions and serve with soy sauce.

6 SERVINGS

*NOTE: As well as enhancing a soup, wontons can be served plain, with vinegar, soy sauce and spiced oil, or with a sweet and sour sauce. In China, soups are eaten between courses. At special festive meals, soup is eaten as the last course.

1 SERVING	
Calories	163
Carbohydrate	16 g
Protein	18 g
Fat	3 g
Fiber	1.6 g
Cholesterol	188 mg

HALIBUT AND FRESH FENNEL SOUP

1 tbsp	butter	15 mL
1	onion, finely diced	1
1	small fennel bulb, thinly sliced	1
2	potatoes, peeled and diced	2
5 cups	fish stock	1.25 L
¾ lb	halibut	350 g
2 tbsp	chopped fresh fennel leaves	30 mL
1 tsp	chopped fresh thyme	5 mL
	salt and freshly ground pepper	

≈ Melt butter in a saucepan. Add onion and sliced fennel; season well. Cook 3 minutes over medium heat. Add potatoes and fish stock; bring to a boil over high heat. Reduce heat to medium and cook about 5 minutes.

≈ Add halibut and cook 7 minutes over medium-low heat or until fish is cooked.

≈ With a slotted spoon, remove fish from soup; discard any skin and bones. Break up flesh into pieces and return to soup. Add fennel leaves and thyme; correct seasoning and serve hot.

6 SERVINGS

*NOTE: HALIBUT IS THE LARGEST OF THE FLAT FISH. IT CAN REACH A LENGTH OF 6 FEET (2 M), AND WEIGH MORE THAN 650 POUNDS (300 KG)!

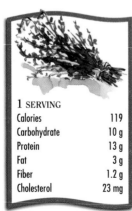

1 SERVING	
Calories	119
Carbohydrate	10 g
Protein	13 g
Fat	3 g
Fiber	1.2 g
Cholesterol	23 mg

*NOTE: OKRA OR 'GUMBO' ORIGINALLY CAME FROM AFRICA AND WAS FIRST INTRODUCED TO THE AMERICAS BY BLACK SLAVES. IT IS A VEGETABLE OFTEN USED IN CARIBBEAN AND CREOLE DISHES.

SEAFOOD GUMBO ~

2 tbsp	butter	30 mL
1	onion, thinly sliced	1
2 cups	sliced fresh okra	500 mL
4 cups	fish stock	1 L
2 tbsp	tomato paste	30 mL
2	fresh thyme sprigs	2
2	fresh parsley sprigs	2
1	bay leaf	1
⅔ lb	shrimp, peeled and deveined	300 g
3 tbsp	olive oil	45 mL
3 tbsp	flour, lightly toasted in oven	45 mL
1 lb	crabmeat	450 g
2	fresh tomatoes, 1 red and 1 yellow, diced	2
2 tbsp	chopped fresh parsley	30 mL
	salt and freshly ground pepper	

~ Melt butter in large saucepan over medium heat. Reduce heat to low, add onion and cook 5 minutes. Add okra and cook 4 more minutes. Add fish stock, tomato paste, thyme and parsley sprigs and bay leaf. Bring to a boil, add shrimp and cook 3 minutes.

~ Combine olive oil and flour; add to the soup and mix well. Reduce heat to medium. Add crabmeat, tomatoes and chopped parsley; let simmer 5 minutes.

~ Correct seasoning and serve hot.

6 SERVINGS

1 SERVING	
Calories	240
Carbohydrate	12 g
Protein	21 g
Fat	12 g
Fiber	2.9 g
Cholesterol	104 mg

VICHYSSOISE WITH MUSSELS

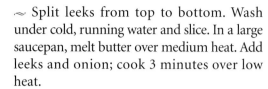

2	leeks, white part only	2
1 tbsp	butter	15 mL
1	onion, thinly sliced	1
4	potatoes, peeled and cubed	4
2	fresh parsley sprigs	2
2 lbs	mussels, scrubbed and bearded	1 kg
1 cup	light cream	250 mL
2 tbsp	chopped fresh parsley	30 mL
	salt and freshly ground pepper	
	parsley sprigs for garnish	

∿ Split leeks from top to bottom. Wash under cold, running water and slice. In a large saucepan, melt butter over medium heat. Add leeks and onion; cook 3 minutes over low heat.

∿ Add potatoes and enough water to cover. Add parsley sprigs and season well. Bring to a boil, reduce heat to medium-low and cook 15 minutes or until potatoes are done.

∿ Meanwhile, place mussels and a little water in a medium saucepan. Cover and cook over high heat until shells open. Discard shells and any unopened mussels. Strain liquid through cheesecloth and set aside.

∿ Purée potato soup in a blender. Add cream, mix and let cool. Add mussels, reserved cooking liquid and chopped parsley. Correct seasoning and serve cold.

6 SERVINGS

∿∿∿∿∿∿∿∿∿∿∿∿∿∿∿∿∿∿∿

*NOTE: VICHYSSOISE WAS CREATED IN THE UNITED STATES BY A FRENCH CHEF. THE NAME IS ALSO GIVEN TO ANY COLD SOUP BASED ON POTATOES AND ANOTHER VEGETABLE, SUCH AS ZUCCHINI.

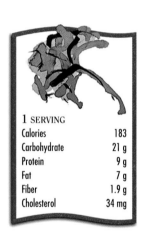

1 SERVING	
Calories	183
Carbohydrate	21 g
Protein	9 g
Fat	7 g
Fiber	1.9 g
Cholesterol	34 mg

JAPANESE MISO SOUP WITH CARP AND SHIITAKE MUSHROOMS

8 cups	water	2 L
¾ cup	dried bonito flakes	175 mL
½	kombu seaweed	½
¾ lb	carp fillets	350 g
1 tbsp	toasted sesame oil	15 mL
1 tbsp	peanut oil	15 mL
¼ lb	sliced shiitake mushrooms	115 g
2	carrots, cut in julienne	2
2 tbsp	chopped ginger	30 mL
2 tbsp	miso*	30 mL
	sea salt and freshly ground pepper	

~ In a large saucepan, bring water to a boil; add bonito flakes and kombu. Let boil a few seconds, or until flakes sink to the bottom. Strain through cheesecloth and return liquid to saucepan.

~ Bring liquid to a boil, reduce heat to medium and add carp fillets and sesame oil. Cook 15 minutes.

~ Meanwhile, heat peanut oil in a pan over high heat and sauté mushrooms 3 minutes. Add carrots and ginger; cook 2 minutes. Add vegetables and miso to soup. Correct seasoning and serve immediately.

6 SERVINGS

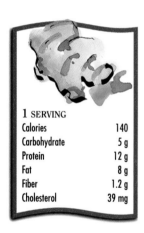

1 SERVING	
Calories	140
Carbohydrate	5 g
Protein	12 g
Fat	8 g
Fiber	1.2 g
Cholesterol	39 mg

Add bonito flakes and kombu seaweed to boiling water.

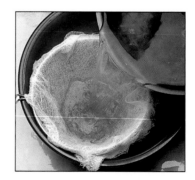

Strain through cheesecloth.

Add carp fillets to cooking liquid.

*NOTE: MISO, A TYPICAL CONDIMENT IN JAPANESE COOKING, IS MADE FROM COOKED SOY BEANS MIXED WITH RICE, BARLEY OR WHEAT GRAINS, AND SALT. THE PASTE IS THEN FERMENTED. THE COLOR OF MISO RANGES FROM WHITE TO DARK BROWN. KOMBU SEAWEED IS A TYPE OF DRIED KELP. WASH WELL BEFORE USING.

Sauté mushrooms, carrots and ginger.

Add vegetables to soup.

Add miso to soup just before serving.

MEDITERRANEAN BOUILLABAISSE

½ cup	extra virgin olive oil	125 mL
2	onions, chopped	2
2	garlic cloves, chopped	2
6	tomatoes, peeled, seeded and chopped	6
1	leek, white part only, sliced	1
1	pinch saffron	1
2	fresh thyme sprigs	2
2	fresh parsley sprigs	2
2	bay leaves	2
1 lb	crayfish	450 g
1 lb	gurnards,* sliced 1 inch (2.5 cm) thick	450 g
4 cups	fish stock	1 L
4	red mullets, sliced 1 inch (2.5 cm) thick	4
½ lb	sea bass fillets	225 g
⅓ cup	chopped fresh parsley	75 mL
	slices of French bread, toasted	
	extra virgin olive oil	
	salt and freshly ground pepper	

~ In a large baking dish, combine olive oil, onions, garlic, tomatoes, leek, saffron, thyme, parsley sprigs and bay leaves. Add crayfish and gurnards; season with pepper and let marinate 2 hours in the refrigerator.

~ Transfer seafood and marinade to a large saucepan; add fish stock and bring to a boil. Cook 8 minutes over medium-high heat. Add red mullet and sea bass; continue cooking 10 minutes.

~ Correct seasoning and add chopped parsley. Serve hot with toasted French bread brushed with olive oil.

6 SERVINGS

*NOTE: BOUILLABAISSE IS A TYPICAL SOUP FROM THE PROVENCE REGION OF FRANCE. BUT THERE EXIST AS MANY VARIETIES OF BOUILLABAISSE AS THERE ARE WAYS OF COMBINING DIFFERENT FISH, EACH ONE AS AUTHENTIC AS THE OTHER.

GURNARDS ARE ARMOR-PLATED, SPINY FISH WITH WINGLIKE PECTORAL FINS. THEY ARE ALSO KNOWN AS SEA ROBINS.

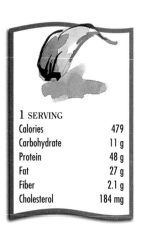

1 SERVING	
Calories	479
Carbohydrate	11 g
Protein	48 g
Fat	27 g
Fiber	2.1 g
Cholesterol	184 mg

SPICY INDONESIAN SNAIL SOUP WITH PAPAYA

2	red chili peppers, seeded and chopped	2
2	garlic cloves	2
2	dry shallots	2
1	2-inch (5 cm) piece fresh ginger, peeled	1
1	2-inch (5 cm) piece fresh turmeric, peeled	1
1 tbsp	coriander seeds	15 mL
2 tbsp	vegetable oil	30 mL
2	large tomatoes, peeled, seeded and chopped	2
5 cups	fish stock	1.25 L
1	lemon grass stalk,* bruised	1
48	canned snails, washed and drained	48
1	ripe papaya, peeled and diced	1
2 tbsp	chopped fresh lemon basil	30 mL
	sea salt	

∼ In a blender, place chili peppers, garlic, shallots, ginger, turmeric, coriander seeds, vegetable oil and tomatoes; purée and set aside.

∼ Pour fish stock into a large saucepan; add lemon grass and bring to a boil. Reduce heat to medium and add spicy purée. Cook 10 minutes. Add snails and cook another 5 minutes.

∼ Add papaya and lemon basil; let simmer 5 minutes. Correct seasoning and serve hot.

6 SERVINGS

∼∼∼∼∼∼∼∼∼∼∼∼∼∼∼∼∼∼∼

*NOTE: TO GET THE MOST FLAVOR OUT OF LEMON GRASS, AN AROMATIC GRASS NATIVE TO SOUTHEAST ASIA, CRUSH THE STIFFEST STALKS BEFORE USING THEM. LEMON GRASS CAN BE KEPT IN THE REFRIGERATOR, WRAPPED IN PLASTIC.

1 SERVING	
Calories	117
Carbohydrate	10 g
Protein	8 g
Fat	5 g
Fiber	1.7 g
Cholesterol	19 mg

*NOTE: CHOOSE CRISP, DARK GREEN SPINACH. FOR IT TO KEEP, IT IS BEST TO WASH AND DRY IT WELL, AND PLACE IT BETWEEN TWO PAPER TOWELS INSIDE A PLASTIC BAG IN THE REFRIGERATOR.

CREAMY OYSTER AND SPINACH SOUP

34	oysters, washed	34
3 tbsp	butter	45 mL
1	onion, finely chopped	1
1	garlic clove, finely chopped	1
¼ tsp	paprika	1 mL
¼ tsp	Cayenne pepper	1 mL
3 tbsp	all-purpose flour	45 mL
½ lb	fresh spinach,* washed and chopped	225 g
1 cup	light cream	250 mL
	freshly ground pepper	

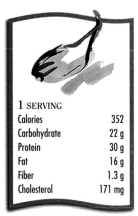

1 SERVING	
Calories	352
Carbohydrate	22 g
Protein	30 g
Fat	16 g
Fiber	1.3 g
Cholesterol	171 mg

≈ Open oysters and carefully remove from shells, reserving water from oysters; set aside. In a heavy saucepan, melt butter over medium heat. Add onion and sauté 4 minutes. Add garlic, paprika and Cayenne pepper; cook 2 minutes.

≈ Add flour and mix well with a wooden spoon; continue cooking 2 minutes. Reduce heat to low. Measure water from oysters, adding more water to make 3 cups (750 mL); add to saucepan and let simmer 3 minutes.

≈ Add spinach and cream. Continue cooking over low heat about 3 minutes, or until spinach is cooked. Add reserved oysters; correct seasoning and serve piping hot.

6 SERVINGS

NEW ENGLAND CLAM CHOWDER

36	fresh medium clams	36
2 tbsp	butter	30 mL
1	onion, diced	1
2 tbsp	flour	30 mL
4 cups	fish stock	1 L
3	potatoes, peeled and diced	3
1	green bell pepper, chopped	1
2	green onions, chopped	2
1 cup	light cream	250 mL
2 tbsp	chopped fresh parsley	30 mL
	salt and freshly ground pepper	

∼ Wash clams and place in a large saucepan with a little water. Cook over medium heat until shells open. Discard any unopened clams and remove shells from the others. Set clams and their juice aside.

∼ In the same saucepan, melt butter. Add onion and sauté 2 minutes over medium heat. Sprinkle in flour and mix well; continue cooking 1 minute. Add fish stock and reserved clam juice. Bring to a boil, season with salt and pepper and add potatoes. Cook over medium heat 12 minutes or until potatoes are done.

∼ Add clams, green pepper and green onions; cook 5 minutes. Add cream and chopped parsley; let simmer 3 minutes and serve.

6 SERVINGS

*NOTE: THERE ARE TWO MAIN TYPES OF CLAM CHOWDER: NEW ENGLAND CLAM CHOWDER AND MANHATTAN CLAM CHOWDER, WHICH USES GROUND TOMATOES INSTEAD OF CREAM.

1 SERVING	
Calories	251
Carbohydrate	18 g
Protein	20 g
Fat	11 g
Fiber	1.5 g
Cholesterol	48 mg

LOBSTER BISQUE

2 lbs	live lobsters	1 kg
2 tbsp	butter	30 mL
1	carrot, diced	1
1	onion, diced	1
2	celery stalks, diced	2
1	leek, white part only, sliced	1
1 tbsp	brandy	15 mL
4 tbsp	white wine	60 mL
6 cups	fish stock	1.5 L
2 tbsp	tomato paste	30 mL
2	fresh tomatoes, cut in 8	2
2	garlic cloves, halved	2
2	fresh thyme sprigs	2
2	fresh parsley sprigs	2
	heavy cream (35% MF) to taste	
	salt and freshly ground pepper	

~ With a chef's knife, split the lobsters into several pieces.

~ In a heavy saucepan, melt the butter over high heat; sauté lobster pieces 2 minutes. Add carrot, onion, celery and leek; cook 5 minutes, stirring constantly. Add brandy and white wine; cook over medium heat to thicken slightly.

~ Add fish stock, tomato paste, tomatoes, garlic, thyme and parsley. Season with salt and pepper and bring to a boil. Cover and cook about 45 minutes over medium heat.

~ Purée soup in a blender and strain through a sieve. If desired, take flesh from lobster claws and tails, break into little pieces and use as garnish.

~ Correct seasoning, stir in cream and serve very hot.

6 SERVINGS

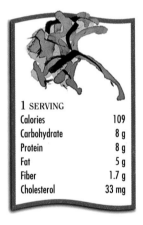

1 SERVING

Calories	109
Carbohydrate	8 g
Protein	8 g
Fat	5 g
Fiber	1.7 g
Cholesterol	33 mg

Sauté lobster in melted butter over high heat.

Add carrot, onion, celery and leek; cook 5 minutes.

Add brandy and white wine.

~~~~~~~~~~~~~~~~

*NOTE: BUY YOUR LOBSTER AT A REPUTABLE FISH STORE. THE LESS TIME IT IS KEPT IN A TANK, THE MORE SAVORY IS ITS FLESH.

Add fish stock, tomato paste, tomatoes, garlic, thyme and parsley.

Purée soup in a blender.

Strain through a sieve.

SINGAPORE SEAFOOD SOUP WITH COCONUT

1	red snapper (about 1 lb/450 g)	1
4	dry shallots	4
4	garlic cloves	4
1	2-inch (5 cm) piece fresh ginger, coarsely chopped	1
2	red chili peppers, seeded	2
2 tbsp	curry powder	30 mL
2 tbsp	vegetable oil	30 mL
1⅔ cups	coconut cream	400 mL
1⅔ cups	fish stock	400 mL
½ lb	fresh shrimp, peeled and deveined	225 g
1 cup	bean sprouts	250 mL
4 tbsp	chopped fresh coriander	60 mL
	sea salt	

∾ Clean fish well and slice into steaks, about 1 inch (2.5 cm) thick. Use the head and the tail to prepare the fish stock.

∾ In a blender, purée shallots, garlic, ginger, chili peppers, curry powder, vegetable oil and ½ cup (125 mL) coconut cream.

∾ In a medium saucepan, combine the remaining coconut cream with fish stock and spicy purée. Cook over medium heat. Season fish steaks with salt and add to saucepan; cook 10 minutes. Add shrimp and bean sprouts; continue cooking 5 minutes.

∾ Add coriander, correct seasoning and serve very hot.

6 SERVINGS

*NOTE: FRESH SHRIMP SMELL OF THE SEA, NOT OF AMMONIA. WASH THEM AND DRAIN THEM WELL, AND THEY WILL KEEP FOR 2 DAYS IN THE REFRIGERATOR.

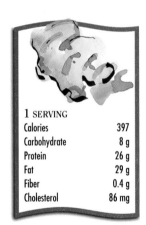

1 SERVING	
Calories	397
Carbohydrate	8 g
Protein	26 g
Fat	29 g
Fiber	0.4 g
Cholesterol	86 mg

Raw, Marinated, Smoked

Dishes made with marinated and smoked fish, or fish

simply 'cooked' in lemon juice, are among the easiest

to prepare, and these international favorites are

surprisingly delicious!

You may have sampled sushi-maki, or savored a

ceviche at a favorite restaurant, not knowing how

easy they are to prepare at home. The following

recipes will convince you to take the next step,

and just a glance at the photos is enough to make

your mouth water!

SCALLOP CARPACCIO WITH ARTICHOKES AND ZUCCHINI

2	zucchini, thinly sliced	2
4	artichoke hearts, thinly sliced	4
2 tbsp	chopped sun-dried tomatoes	30 mL
1 tbsp	chopped fresh thyme	15 mL
16	fresh scallops	16
2 tbsp	extra virgin olive oil	30 mL
1 tbsp	balsamic vinegar	15 mL
	juice of 1 lemon	
	sea salt and freshly ground pepper	

~ Blanch zucchini, drain well and place in a bowl. Add artichoke hearts, sun-dried tomatoes and thyme; season and mix well. Set aside.

~ Slice scallops very thin and divide among plates. Sprinkle with olive oil, balsamic vinegar and lemon juice; season with salt and pepper. Place artichoke and zucchini salad in the center of each plate. Serve immediately.

4 SERVINGS

*NOTE: CARPACCIO IS AN ITALIAN APPETIZER MADE WITH SLICES OF RAW BEEF DRIZZLED WITH AN OLIVE OIL VINAIGRETTE AND SERVED WITH THINLY SLICED ONION.

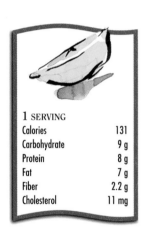

1 SERVING	
Calories	131
Carbohydrate	9 g
Protein	8 g
Fat	7 g
Fiber	2.2 g
Cholesterol	11 mg

*NOTE: GRAVLAX, OR
SWEDISH-STYLE MARINATED
SALMON, FREEZES WELL
WHEN TOPPED WITH OLIVE OIL
IN AN AIRTIGHT CONTAINER.

GRAVLAX

1	**3 lb (1.5 kg) fresh salmon fillet with skin**	1
4 tbsp	**coarse salt**	60 mL
3 tbsp	**sugar**	45 mL
2 tbsp	**crushed peppercorns**	30 mL
1 cup	**chopped fresh dill**	250 mL
1	**cucumber, slivered**	1
1	**lemon, sliced, cut in wedges**	1
8	**slices rye bread**	8

~ Carefully remove bones from salmon.

~ Combine salt, sugar and pepper; sprinkle over salmon. Cover salmon with chopped dill. Place fillet on large plate or tray and cover with aluminum foil. Put weight on the salmon so that it is being pressed down, and keep it in the refrigerator for 3 days, turning it over every 12 hours.

~ Slice salmon and serve on small rye bread canapés with slivers of cucumber. Garnish with lemon.

4 SERVINGS

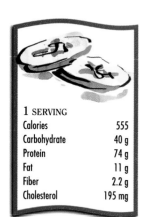

1 SERVING	
Calories	555
Carbohydrate	40 g
Protein	74 g
Fat	11 g
Fiber	2.2 g
Cholesterol	195 mg

TARAMASALATA

½ lb	smoked cod roe	225 g
2	garlic cloves, minced	2
5	slices white bread, crusts removed	5
1 cup	milk	250 mL
1 cup	olive oil	250 mL
4 tbsp	fresh lemon juice	60 mL
2 tbsp	wine vinegar	30 mL
	toasted bread	
	Kalamata olives (optional)	
	freshly ground pepper	

≈ Crush fish roe and add garlic. Soak bread in milk, and squeeze out excess liquid. Add bread to fish roe and mix well.

≈ With a whisk, gradually add olive oil and beat until mixture is thick. Add lemon juice, vinegar and pepper to taste; mix well. Refrigerate and serve cold, spread over toasted bread and with Kalamata olives.

4 SERVINGS

*NOTE: TARAMASALATA IS A GREEK SPECIALTY OFTEN SERVED WITH BREAD AS AN APPETIZER.

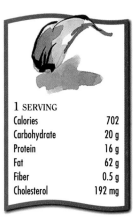

1 SERVING	
Calories	702
Carbohydrate	20 g
Protein	16 g
Fat	62 g
Fiber	0.5 g
Cholesterol	192 mg

Sushi Rice

2 cups	short grain sushi rice	500 mL
2¼ cups	water	550 mL
1	3-inch (7.5 cm) square kombu seaweed	1
4 tbsp	sake or mirin (rice wine)	60 mL
4 tbsp	rice vinegar	60 mL
2 tbsp	sugar	30 mL
2 tsp	sea salt	10 mL

~ Rinse rice under cold, running water for 20 minutes. Drain well and place rice in a heavy saucepan; add water, kombu and sake. Bring to a boil, remove kombu and reduce heat to low. Cover and cook about 15 minutes, or until all the liquid has been absorbed. Do not stir during cooking process.

~ Remove pan from heat and let cool 15 minutes. Using wooden spoon, gently stir rice. Cover with a towel and let stand 10 minutes.

~ Combine vinegar, sugar and salt and pour over rice. Toss rice gently until it cools to room temperature. Cover with a damp towel and set aside at room temperature until ready to use.

MAKES ABOUT 4 CUPS (1L)

Maki-Sushi

~

4	sheets nori seaweed*	4
1 cup	cooked sushi rice (see recipe above)	250 mL
1½ oz	fresh salmon	45 g
2½ oz	fresh tuna	75 g
2½ oz	fresh crabmeat	75 g
	avocado, green onion, cucumber, red and yellow bell pepper	
	soy sauce	
	marinated ginger slices	
	wasabi paste	

~ Use a whole sheet or ½ sheet of seaweed, depending on the size of rolls desired. Place the sheet on a makisu (bamboo mat). Wet the tips of your fingers and spread rice over seaweed, leaving 1 inch (2.5 cm) at either end.

~ Place desired garnishes in center, and roll using the makisu. Press down to seal. Slice the rolls with a wet knife. Serve with soy sauce, marinated ginger and wasabi.

4 SERVINGS

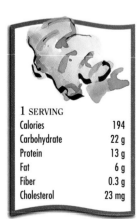

1 SERVING	
Calories	194
Carbohydrate	22 g
Protein	13 g
Fat	6 g
Fiber	0.3 g
Cholesterol	23 mg

~~~~~~~~~~~~~

*NOTE: NORI SEAWEED
IS RICH IN CALCIUM,
PHOSPHOROUS, IRON, IODINE
AND VITAMIN A. IT IS
COMPRESSED INTO SPECKLED
SHEETS, RANGING IN COLOR
FROM BROWN TO DARK
GREEN.

*Spread the rice over the
seaweed.*

*Place garnishes in center; roll
using the makisu.*

Press down to seal the roll.

NIGIRI-SUSHI

2½ cups	cooked sushi rice (see recipe page 60)	625 mL
1	sheet nori seaweed	1
4 tbsp	salmon roe	60 mL
8	large shrimp, cooked and peeled	8
⅓ lb	fresh red tuna, cut into 8 strips	150 g
⅓ lb	fresh bonito, cut into 8 strips	150 g
1	green onion, thinly sliced	1
1 tbsp	wasabi powder*	15 mL
	marinated ginger slices	
	soy sauce	
	black radish sprouts	

≈ Moisten hands and mold 2 tbsp (30 mL) sushi rice into an oval shaped ball. You should be able to make 28 balls in total.

≈ Cut nori sheet into 1 x 7 inch rectangles (2.5 x 17.5 cm). Roll each rectangle around a ball of rice. The seaweed should come higher than the rice so you can top the rice with 1 tbsp (15 mL) of salmon roe.

≈ On each of the remaining balls of rice, place 1 strip of fish or shrimp. Press gently but firmly to keep fish in place. Garnish with green onion.

≈ Mix wasabi powder with enough hot water to make a thick paste. Serve nigiri-sushi with wasabi paste, marinated ginger slices and soy sauce. Accompany with black radish sprouts.

4 SERVINGS

*NOTE: WASABI IS A ROOT, OF THE HORSERADISH FAMILY. IT HAS A STRONG FLAVOR AND IS SERVED WITH SUSHI AND SASHIMI. DRIED AND GROUND, IT IS SOLD EITHER AS A POWDER OR A PASTE. IT IS ONLY FOUND FRESH IN JAPAN.

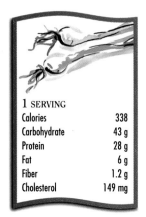

1 SERVING	
Calories	338
Carbohydrate	43 g
Protein	28 g
Fat	6 g
Fiber	1.2 g
Cholesterol	149 mg

FRESH CILANTRO CEVICHE

1 lb	haddock fillets	450 g
⅓ cup	fresh lime juice	75 mL
⅔ cup	olive oil	150 mL
1	red chili pepper, seeded and finely chopped	1
1	red onion, thinly sliced	1
1	garlic clove, finely chopped	1
2 tbsp	chopped fresh cilantro	30 mL
1	green bell pepper, thinly sliced	1
12	cherry tomatoes, quartered	12
	sea salt and freshly ground pepper	
	tortilla corn chips	

∼ Cut fish across the grain into fine strips; place in a baking dish. Pour lime juice over fish, season with salt and pepper and let marinate 15 minutes.

∼ In a bowl, combine olive oil, chili pepper, onion, garlic and cilantro. Pour over fish. Garnish with green pepper and cherry tomatoes and serve immediately. Accompany with corn chips.

4 SERVINGS

*NOTE: TO KEEP CILANTRO FRESH AS LONG AS POSSIBLE, STAND THE STALKS UP IN A CONTAINER WITH A BIT OF WATER, COVER IT WITH A PLASTIC BAG AND REFRIGERATE.

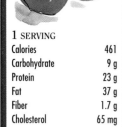

1 SERVING	
Calories	461
Carbohydrate	9 g
Protein	23 g
Fat	37 g
Fiber	1.7 g
Cholesterol	65 mg

*NOTE: SOAKED IN OLIVE OIL (FLAVORED WITH GARLIC, BAY LEAVES OR OTHER HERBS), GRILLED PEPPERS WILL KEEP UP TO 2 WEEKS IN THE REFRIGERATOR.

FRESH TUNA CARPACCIO WITH ROASTED BELL PEPPERS ∼

1	green bell pepper, halved	1
1	yellow bell pepper, halved	1
1 tbsp	olive oil	15 mL
1 lb	fresh tuna, very thinly sliced	450 g
3 tbsp	extra virgin olive oil	45 mL
2 tbsp	chopped fresh chives	30 mL
2 tbsp	black olive purée	30 mL
	juice of ½ lemon	
	juice of ½ lime	
	whole Parmesan cheese	
	sea salt and freshly ground pepper	
	fresh chervil sprigs for garnish	

∼ Preheat oven to 400°F (200°C).

∼ Place bell pepper halves on a baking sheet, cut side down. Brush with olive oil and cook 15 minutes in oven. Let cool in a bowl covered with plastic wrap; peel. Cut each piece in half.

∼ Place one piece of green pepper and one piece of yellow pepper in the center of each plate. Place 3 slices of tuna around the peppers. Sprinkle with olive oil and lemon and lime juice. Season with salt and pepper. Top with fresh chives; garnish with olive purée, Parmesan (shaved with a paring knife) and a sprig of chervil.

4 SERVINGS

1 SERVING	
Calories	300
Carbohydrate	6 g
Protein	24 g
Fat	20 g
Fiber	0.9 g
Cholesterol	38 mg

SINGAPORE TEA-SMOKED RED SNAPPER

2 cups	ice water	500 mL
4 tbsp	soy sauce	60 mL
2 tbsp	brown sugar	30 mL
¼ tsp	salt	1 mL
⅓ cup	finely chopped fresh ginger	75 mL
2	red snapper fillets, about ½ lb (225 g) each	2
4 tbsp	Chinese black tea*	60 mL
4	star anise pods, crushed	4
2	cinnamon sticks, crushed	2
¼ cup	uncooked rice	50 mL
4	garlic cloves, halved	4
4	cardamom pods	4
2 tbsp	coriander seeds	30 mL

~ In a baking dish, combine water, soy sauce, brown sugar, salt and ginger. Place fish in dish and let marinate 3 hours. Remove fish, drain and pat dry with paper towels; set aside.

~ In a wok over medium-low heat, mix together black tea, star anise, cinnamon, rice, garlic, cardamom and coriander. Place fish on a grill or in a bamboo steamer inside the wok, about 2 inches (5 cm) above smoking mixture.

~ Cover the wok and smoke fish for 40 minutes, or until fish has turned a light-brown color. Let cool and serve.

4 SERVINGS

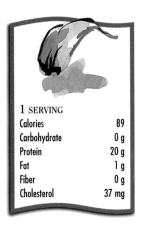

1 SERVING	
Calories	89
Carbohydrate	0 g
Protein	20 g
Fat	1 g
Fiber	0 g
Cholesterol	37 mg

Combine water, soy sauce, brown sugar, salt and ginger.

Place fish in marinade.

Dry marinated fish with paper towels.

*NOTE: SMOKING FOODS WITH TEA IS A VERY POPULAR TECHNIQUE IN SINGAPORE AND PARTS OF CHINA.

In a wok, mix together black tea, star anise, cinnamon, rice, garlic, cardamom and coriander.

Place fish on a grill, inside the wok.

Cover the wok and smoke the fish.

*NOTE: THERE ARE TWO TECHNIQUES FOR SMOKING SALMON: IN HOT SMOKING, IT IS EXPOSED TO HOT AIR FROM A FAST-BURNING FIRE, THEN PLACED IN THE THICK SMOKE FROM A FIRE COVERED WITH SAWDUST, FOR 6 TO 12 HOURS. IN COLD SMOKING, IT IS EXPOSED TO THE SMOKE FROM A SLOW-BURNING FIRE, FOR 1 TO 3 WEEKS, DEPENDING ON THE SIZE OF THE FISH.

SMOKED SALMON MOUSSE CANAPÉS ~

6 oz	smoked salmon	175 g
1 cup	heavy cream (35% MF)	250 mL
2 tbsp	chopped fresh chives	30 mL
	salt and freshly ground pepper	
	chopped red bell pepper	
	chopped fresh chives	
	capers	
	crackers	

~ Purée smoked salmon in a blender or food processor. Add cream and blend. Transfer to a bowl, add chives and season to taste.

~ Place mousse in a pastry bag, and squeeze onto crackers. Garnish with red pepper, chives and capers. Serve immediately.

4 SERVINGS

1 SERVING	
Calories	260
Carbohydrate	2 g
Protein	9 g
Fat	24 g
Fiber	0.1 g
Cholesterol	91 mg

SALMON AND SCALLOP TARTARE WITH CHERVIL

2	dry shallots, finely chopped	2
1 tsp	Dijon mustard	5 mL
1 tbsp	lime juice	15 mL
3 tbsp	olive oil	45 mL
⅔ lb	fresh salmon	300 g
½ lb	scallops	225 g
3 tbsp	chopped fresh chervil	45 mL
½	red bell pepper, finely diced	½
½	yellow bell pepper, finely diced	½
2 tbsp	basil oil (see recipe page 252)	30 mL
	salt and freshly ground pepper	
	fresh chervil for garnish	

∽ To prepare the vinaigrette, in a large bowl, combine the shallots and mustard. Add lime juice and season with salt and pepper. With a whisk, gradually mix in olive oil.

∽ Chop salmon and scallops into small dice; drizzle with vinaigrette and mix well. Add chopped chervil, correct seasoning and divide mixture among plates. Place bell peppers around the seafood, sprinkle with basil oil and garnish with fresh chervil. Serve immediately.

4 SERVINGS

*NOTE: IT IS THE CITRIC ACID FOUND IN THE LIME JUICE THAT 'COOKS' THE FISH.

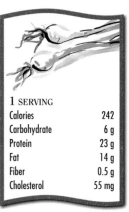

1 SERVING	
Calories	242
Carbohydrate	6 g
Protein	23 g
Fat	14 g
Fiber	0.5 g
Cholesterol	55 mg

SMOKED SALMON BLINIS

1 tbsp	active dry yeast	15 mL
1 tsp	sugar	5 mL
2 cups	warm milk	500 mL
1 cup	buckwheat flour	250 mL
1 cup	all-purpose flour	250 mL
1 tsp	salt	5 mL
2	eggs	2
4 tbsp	sour cream	60 mL
1 cup	yogurt	250 mL
1 tbsp	butter	15 mL
1 lb	smoked salmon	450 g
2 tbsp	salmon roe	30 mL
2 tbsp	lumpfish roe	30 mL
	fresh dill sprigs	
	freshly ground pepper	

~ In a small bowl, mix together yeast, sugar and ¼ cup (50 mL) of warm milk. Cover and let stand about 10 minutes, or until frothy.

~ In a large bowl, combine buckwheat flour, all-purpose flour and salt. Add remaining warm milk, yeast mixture and eggs. Mix well and let stand in a warm place for 15 minutes. Meanwhile, mix together sour cream and yogurt; season with pepper and set aside.

~ Heat butter in a frying pan over medium heat. Pour in ¼ cup (50 mL) of batter and cook until bubbles appear on surface. Flip the blini and cook until golden.

~ To serve, place 1 blini in the center of each plate; garnish with smoked salmon and a spoonful of yogurt and cream mixture. Cover with a second blini. Serve with salmon and lumpfish roe and garnish with a sprig of fresh dill.

4 SERVINGS

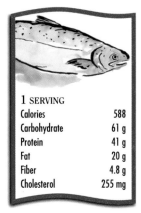

1 SERVING	
Calories	588
Carbohydrate	61 g
Protein	41 g
Fat	20 g
Fiber	4.8 g
Cholesterol	255 mg

Mix together yeast, sugar and ¼ cup (50 mL) of warm milk.

To the flour and salt mixture, add remaining warm milk, yeast mixture and eggs.

Cook blinis until bubbles appear on surface.

~~~~~~~~~~~~~

*NOTE: TO PREVENT BLINIS FROM STICKING TOGETHER, SEPARATE THEM WITH SHEETS OF WAX PAPER.

Garnish each blini with smoked salmon.

Top with a spoonful of the yogurt and cream mixture.

Cover with a second blini.

SASHIMI

⅓ lb	daikon radish, cut in julienne	150 g
⅓ lb	carrots, cut in julienne	150 g
1 tbsp	wasabi powder	15 mL
½ lb	yellowtail tuna fillets, cut in 12 pieces	225 g
½ lb	salmon fillets, cut in 12 pieces	225 g
½ lb	mackerel fillets, cut in 12 pieces	225 g
	lettuce leaves	
	marinated ginger slices*	
	soy sauce	

≈ Soak daikon and carrot in very cold water for 1 hour.

≈ Mix wasabi powder with enough hot water to make a thick paste.

≈ Place 3 pieces of each kind of fish on each plate. Drain daikon and carrot well, and place on each plate, along with lettuce. Serve with wasabi paste, marinated ginger and soy sauce.

4 SERVINGS

*NOTE: GINGER MARINATED WITH VINEGAR IS THE ESSENTIAL JAPANESE CONDIMENT FOR SUSHI. IT IS EATEN BETWEEN COURSES, TO CLEAN THE PALATE AND FRESHEN THE BREATH. IT ALSO HAS CERTAIN ANTIBIOTIC PROPERTIES.

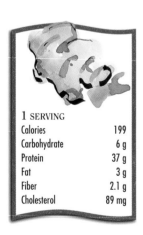

1 SERVING	
Calories	199
Carbohydrate	6 g
Protein	37 g
Fat	3 g
Fiber	2.1 g
Cholesterol	89 mg

~~~~~~~~~~~~~~~

*NOTE: THE TERM
'FLORENTINE' IS USED TO
DESCRIBE MANY FISH, WHITE
MEAT AND EGG DISHES
PREPARED WITH SPINACH
AND, VERY OFTEN, WITH
MORNAY SAUCE.

SMOKED SALMON FLORENTINE ~

½ lb	fresh spinach	225 g
16	slices smoked salmon	16
1	recipe smoked salmon mousse (see page 68)	1
1	red onion, finely chopped	1
	juice of 1 lemon	
	freshly ground pepper	
	capers	
	extra virgin olive oil	

~ Remove stalks and wash spinach; place in a pot with a little water, cover and cook about 2 minutes. Drain well and let cool.

~ On a cutting board, arrange 4 slices of salmon so that they overlap slightly. Spread salmon mousse on each and top with spinach.

~ Roll the slices into a cylinder and press it together to keep its form. Repeat this technique with remaining smoked salmon to make 4 rolls. Refrigerate 1 hour. With a sharp knife, slice the rolls.

~ Season rolls with pepper, sprinkle with lemon juice and serve with chopped red onion, capers and olive oil.

4 SERVINGS

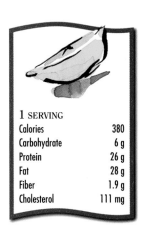

1 SERVING	
Calories	380
Carbohydrate	6 g
Protein	26 g
Fat	28 g
Fiber	1.9 g
Cholesterol	111 mg

DEEP-FRIED

Deep-frying is one of the best and easiest ways to cook

fish and seafood. Dipped in a delicate batter and

plunged into a bath of boiling oil, the flesh cooks

rapidly and retains its full flavor.

Adults and children alike are sure to enjoy sinking

their teeth into these delicious, golden treats.

SHRIMP, FISH AND VEGETABLE TEMPURA

2	eggs	2
1¾ cups	cold water	425 mL
¼ tsp	salt	1 mL
2 cups	all-purpose flour	500 mL
8 oz	turbot fillets, cut into strips	250 g
8 oz	bonito fillets, cut into strips	250 g
8	large shrimp, peeled and deveined	8
2	carrots, sliced diagonally	2
1	zucchini, sliced diagonally	1
8	flat green beans, sliced in 3	8
	soy sauce and dashi sauce (see recipe page 252)	
	peanut oil for deep-frying	

≈ Preheat peanut oil in deep-fryer to 340°F (170°C).

≈ Beat eggs, and stir in cold water with chopsticks. Add salt and gradually stir in flour. Do not mix too much or batter will become sticky.

≈ Rinse and pat dry fish strips with paper towels; season well. Dip strips in batter and deep-fry in hot oil. Repeat with shrimp, carrots, zucchini and green beans. Tempura is ready when it rises to the surface and is lightly golden.

≈ Carefully remove and drain on paper towels. Serve with a mixture of equal amounts of soy sauce and dashi sauce.

4 SERVINGS

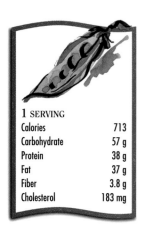

1 SERVING	
Calories	713
Carbohydrate	57 g
Protein	38 g
Fat	37 g
Fiber	3.8 g
Cholesterol	183 mg

*NOTE: TEMPURA IS A JAPANESE TECHNIQUE FOR PREPARING FISH AND VEGETABLE FRITTERS. THE OIL IS TOO HOT WHEN THE FRITTERS RISE IMMEDIATELY TO THE SURFACE. IF THE FRITTERS STAY ON THE BOTTOM, THE OIL IS NOT HOT ENOUGH.

Stir cold water into beaten eggs with chopsticks.

Gradually stir in flour.

Dip fish, shrimp and vegetables in batter.

SHRIMP FRITTERS WITH CORIANDER

½ lb	shrimp, peeled and deveined	225 g
1 cup	all-purpose flour	250 mL
4 tbsp	chopped fresh coriander	60 mL
3	garlic cloves, chopped	3
2 tbsp	chopped fresh ginger	30 mL
1	egg	1
¾ cup	coconut cream	175 mL
	salt and freshly ground pepper	
	peanut oil for deep-frying	
	soy sauce	
	alfalfa sprouts	

≈ Preheat peanut oil in deep-fryer to 350°F (180°C).

≈ Finely chop shrimp and place in a bowl. Add flour, coriander, garlic and ginger; mix well. Beat egg and add coconut cream. Pour into shrimp mixture; season and mix well.

≈ Deep-fry spoonfuls of mixture in hot oil for about 5 minutes, or until fritters are golden and puffy.

≈ Serve with soy sauce and alfalfa sprouts.

4 SERVINGS

*NOTE: BECAUSE EGG SHELLS ABSORB ODORS, IT IS IMPORTANT TO KEEP EGGS IN A CARDBOARD OR PLASTIC CONTAINER IN THE REFRIGERATOR.

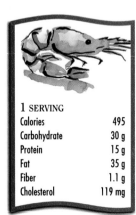

1 SERVING	
Calories	495
Carbohydrate	30 g
Protein	15 g
Fat	35 g
Fiber	1.1 g
Cholesterol	119 mg

~~~~~~~~~~~~

*NOTE: KEEP LIVE CRABS IN A PAPER BAG IN THE REFRIGERATOR OR IN A COOLER. THEY WILL DIE IF SUBMERGED IN WATER OR PLACED ON ICE. COOK THEM WITHIN 24 HOURS.

DEEP-FRIED SOFT-SHELLED CRABS ~

8	fresh soft-shelled blue crabs*	8
1 cup	breadcrumbs	250 mL
½ cup	cornmeal	125 mL
2	eggs, beaten	2
3 tbsp	heavy cream (35% MF)	45 mL
	peanut oil for deep-frying	
	lemon wedges	
	salt	

~ Place crabs in boiling salted water and cook 3 minutes, or until pink. Remove, drain and pat dry with paper towels.

~ Preheat oil in deep-fryer to 340°F (170°C).

~ Combine breadcrumbs and cornmeal. Mix beaten eggs and cream together. Dip crabs in beaten egg mixture, then dredge in breadcrumb mixture.

~ Deep-fry in hot oil until golden brown on both sides. Drain on paper towels and serve with lemon wedges.

4 SERVINGS

1 SERVING	
Calories	668
Carbohydrate	30 g
Protein	47 g
Fat	40 g
Fiber	2.1 g
Cholesterol	318 mg

GOLDEN FRIED OYSTERS WITH TARTAR SAUCE ～

24	fresh oysters	24
2	eggs, beaten	2
¼ cup	light cream	50 mL
1 cup	breadcrumbs	250 mL
¼ cup	chopped fresh chives	50 mL
½ cup	all-purpose flour	125 mL
	peanut oil for deep-frying	
	tartar sauce (see recipe page 253)	
	lemon slices for garnish	

～ Wash oysters under cold, running water and remove shells (as shown on page 11). Mix eggs with cream. Combine breadcrumbs and chives.

～ Preheat oil in deep-fryer to 350°F (180°C). Coat oysters in flour, dip in egg mixture, then dredge in breadcrumbs.

～ Deep-fry oysters in hot oil 3 minutes or until golden brown. Drain on paper towels and serve with tartar sauce and lemon slices.

4 SERVINGS

*NOTE: PEANUT OIL IS ONE OF THE BEST OILS TO USE FOR DEEP-FRYING. IT CAN BE HEATED TO UP TO 400°F (200°C).

1 SERVING	
Calories	606
Carbohydrate	47 g
Protein	37 g
Fat	30 g
Fiber	1.1 g
Cholesterol	267 mg

RED SNAPPER AND SPINACH WONTONS

1 tbsp	vegetable oil	15 mL
2	dry shallots, chopped	2
2 cups	chopped fresh spinach	500 mL
½ lb	red snapper fillets, diced	225 g
½ lb	crabmeat	225 g
2 tbsp	soy sauce	30 mL
1 tbsp	brown sugar	15 mL
1 lb	wonton wrappers	450 g
	freshly ground pepper	
	peanut oil for deep-frying	

≈ Heat vegetable oil in a medium frying pan and sauté shallots 2 minutes over low heat. Add spinach and cook 1 minute or until wilted. Place in a medium bowl. Add snapper, crabmeat, soy sauce, brown sugar and pepper to taste; mix well.

≈ Preheat peanut oil in deep-fryer to 350°F (180°C).

≈ Place one tablespoon (15 mL) of fish filling on each wonton wrapper. Brush edges with water and fold corners in, pressing together to seal.

≈ Fry wontons in hot oil until golden.

≈ Serve with a hot chili pepper sauce, or sauce of your choice.

4 SERVINGS

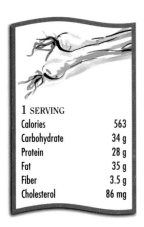

1 SERVING	
Calories	563
Carbohydrate	34 g
Protein	28 g
Fat	35 g
Fiber	3.5 g
Cholesterol	86 mg

Cook spinach until wilted.

Add red snapper, crabmeat, soy sauce and brown sugar.

Place one tablespoon (15 mL) of filling on each wonton wrapper.

DEEP-FRIED

*NOTE: CHOOSE FIRM SHALLOTS WITH A DRY SKIN. WRAP PEELED BULBS IN PLASTIC AND KEEP IN THE REFRIGERATOR. THEY LOSE THEIR FLAVOR AFTER 24 HOURS.

Brush edges with water.

Fold opposite corners in towards the center.

Fold in the other 2 corners and press together to seal.

JAPANESE SALMON AND TOFU BALLS

¾ lb	salmon fillets	350 g
½ lb	tofu	225 g
¼ cup	all-purpose flour	50 mL
2 tbsp	chopped fresh garlic chives	30 mL
¼ cup	soy sauce	50 mL
	marinated ginger slices	
	salt and freshly ground pepper	
	peanut oil for deep-frying	
	extra flour	

≈ Place salmon in a medium saucepan and cover with salted water. Bring to a boil over medium-high heat. Reduce heat and simmer about 3 minutes. Drain; remove skin and bones. Flake salmon and chop finely.

≈ Cut tofu into ½ inch (1 cm) squares and cook 2 minutes in salted, boiling water. Drain well and transfer to a clean cheesecloth; squeeze to remove excess liquid. Place tofu in bowl and mash with a fork. Add salmon, flour and garlic chives. Season and mix well.

≈ Preheat oil in deep-fryer to 350°F (180°C).

≈ Form salmon mixture into balls. Roll in flour and deep-fry in hot oil until golden. Serve with soy sauce and marinated ginger.

4 SERVINGS

*NOTE: TOFU (OR BEANCURD) IS MADE FROM SOY BEANS THAT ARE FIRST SOAKED AND PURÉED THEN BOILED AND SIEVED. SOAKED IN WATER, IT WILL KEEP 5 DAYS IN THE REFRIGERATOR. THE WATER SHOULD BE CHANGED DAILY.

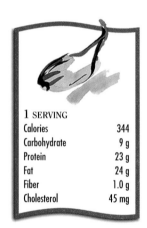

1 SERVING	
Calories	344
Carbohydrate	9 g
Protein	23 g
Fat	24 g
Fiber	1.0 g
Cholesterol	45 mg

CRISPY FRIED MACKEREL AND SARDINES

8	fresh sardines	8
8 oz	mackerel fillets	250 g
½ cup	dashi (see recipe page 252)	125 mL
¼ cup	soy sauce	50 mL
¼ cup	rice vinegar	50 mL
½	red chili pepper, seeded and diced	½
½ cup	all-purpose flour	125 mL
2	eggs, beaten with 2 tbsp (30 mL) water	2
1 cup	sesame seeds*	250 mL
1 cup	chopped cashew nuts*	250 mL
	peanut oil for deep-frying	
	salt and freshly ground pepper	

≈ Prepare sardines as shown on page 10. Spread fish out flat, rinse under cold, running water and pat dry. Cut mackerel fillets into cubes and set aside.

≈ To prepare the dipping sauce, combine dashi, soy sauce, rice vinegar and chili pepper.

≈ Preheat oil in deep-fryer to 350°F (180°C). Season sardines and mackerel with salt and pepper. Dip in flour, then in eggs and coat each piece with either sesame seeds or cashews.

≈ Deep-fry in hot oil until golden brown and drain on paper towels. Serve with dipping sauce.

4 SERVINGS

*NOTE: FOR A VARIATION, MIX TOASTED AND NON-TOASTED SESAME SEEDS, OR USE PINE NUTS OR PISTACHIOS INSTEAD OF CASHEWS.

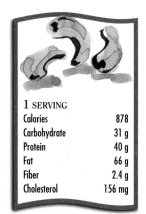

1 SERVING	
Calories	878
Carbohydrate	31 g
Protein	40 g
Fat	66 g
Fiber	2.4 g
Cholesterol	156 mg

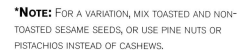

CRAB SPRING ROLLS WITH SWEET AND SOUR SAUCE

SWEET AND SOUR SAUCE

4 tbsp	brown sugar	60 mL
4 tbsp	rice vinegar	60 mL
½ cup	chicken broth	125 mL
2 tbsp	soy sauce	30 mL
2 tbsp	fish sauce (nam pla)	30 mL
1 tbsp	chopped fresh ginger	15 mL
1 tbsp	tomato paste	15 mL
1 tbsp	cornstarch	15 mL

SPRING ROLLS

½ lb	crabmeat	225 g
1 cup	bean sprouts	250 mL
2	carrots, cut in julienne	2
2	garlic cloves, finely chopped	2
1 tbsp	fish sauce (nam pla)	15 mL
2 tbsp	chopped fresh lemon basil	30 mL
2 tbsp	chopped fresh mint	30 mL
8	rice paper wrappers (7 inches/17.5 cm in diameter)	8
	peanut oil for deep-frying	
	fresh spinach and carrot julienne	

~ In a small saucepan, mix together all sweet and sour sauce ingredients, except cornstarch, and bring to a boil. Dilute cornstarch in 2 tbsp (30 mL) water; add to sauce and cook about 3 minutes.

~ In a medium bowl, mix together crabmeat, bean sprouts, carrots, garlic, fish sauce, basil and mint. Set filling aside.

~ Preheat oil in deep-fryer to 375°F (190°C).

~ Dip a rice paper wrapper in hot water for 20 seconds, or until it is soft. Spread out on work surface and place a small amount of filling in the center. Fold wrapper over the filling and fold in ends before rolling. Repeat with the other wrappers.

~ Deep-fry rolls in hot oil until they are crispy and lightly golden. Serve with sweet and sour sauce, and fresh spinach and carrot julienne.

4 SERVINGS

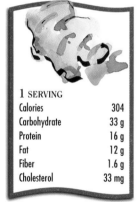

1 SERVING	
Calories	304
Carbohydrate	33 g
Protein	16 g
Fat	12 g
Fiber	1.6 g
Cholesterol	33 mg

Dilute cornstarch in water and add to sweet and sour sauce.

Mix together crabmeat, bean sprouts, carrots, garlic, fish sauce, basil and mint.

Dip a rice paper wrapper in hot water.

DEEP-FRIED

~~~~~~~~~~~~~~

*NOTE: RICE PAPER
WRAPPERS ARE MADE WITH
FLOUR, SALT AND WATER,
MIXED INTO A PASTE. THEY
ARE COOKED BETWEEN HOT
IRONS AND DRIED.

*Place a small amount of filling
in the center.*

*Fold wrapper over the filling
and fold in ends.*

Roll.

FISH AND VEGETABLE CHIPS

1 cup	all-purpose flour	250 mL
1 tsp	salt	5 mL
1 tsp	baking soda	5 mL
1½ cups	buttermilk	375 mL
1	egg, beaten	1
1	taro,* peeled and thinly sliced	1
1	lotus,* peeled and thinly sliced	1
1	sweet potato, peeled and thinly sliced	1
1	beet, peeled and thinly sliced	1
1 lb	fresh cod	450 g
	peanut oil for deep frying	
	salt and freshly ground pepper	
	tartar sauce (see recipe page 253)	

~ Mix together flour, salt and baking soda. Add buttermilk and beaten egg; mix well and set aside.

~ Preheat oil in deep-fryer to 350°F (180°C). Deep-fry taro, lotus and sweet potato until golden and crispy; set aside. Deep-fry beet slices until crispy, about 2 minutes on each side; set aside.

~ Cut cod into 4 inch (10 cm) pieces and season well. Dip in reserved batter and deep-fry about 2 minutes, or until crispy and golden. Drain on paper towels. Serve with tartar sauce and vegetable chips.

4 SERVINGS

*NOTE: TARO IS A TUBER THAT CAN BE COOKED IN THE SAME WAY AS POTATOES. LOTUS IS NATIVE TO THE FAR EAST. THE CUT ROOT HAS HOLES, WHICH GIVES THIS VEGETABLE A DECORATIVE QUALITY.

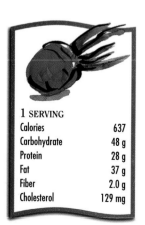

1 SERVING	
Calories	637
Carbohydrate	48 g
Protein	28 g
Fat	37 g
Fiber	2.0 g
Cholesterol	129 mg

*NOTE: THE LARGEST CLAM ON RECORD WAS DISCOVERED NEAR OKINAWA, JAPAN. IT WEIGHED ABOUT 750 LBS (340 KG)!

SPICY CLAM FRITTERS WITH HERB MAYONNAISE

4 lbs	fresh medium clams	1.8 kg
½ cup	dry white wine	125 mL
1	fresh thyme sprig	1
2	fresh parsley sprigs	2
2 cups	all-purpose flour	500 mL
½ tsp	paprika	2 mL
½ tsp	Cayenne pepper	2 mL
2	eggs, beaten	2
2	red chili peppers, seeded and finely chopped	2
	milk	
	herb mayonnaise (see recipe page 250)	
	peanut oil for deep-frying	

∼ Wash clams and place in a large saucepan. Add wine and herbs. Cover and cook over high heat about 5 minutes, until shells open. Discard any clams that do not open.

∼ Remove shells and strain clam juice through a sieve; add enough milk to make 1 cup (250 mL) and set aside. Finely chop clams and add flour, paprika and Cayenne pepper.

∼ Combine eggs with reserved clam juice and milk mixture; add to clams. Add chili peppers and mix well.

∼ Preheat oil in deep-fryer to 350°F (180°C). Drop spoonfuls of clam mixture in hot oil and fry until they are golden and puffy. Drain on paper towels and serve with herb mayonnaise.

4 SERVINGS

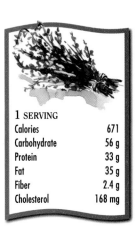

1 SERVING	
Calories	671
Carbohydrate	56 g
Protein	33 g
Fat	35 g
Fiber	2.4 g
Cholesterol	168 mg

FRITTO MISTO DI MARE

1 cup	all-purpose flour	250 mL
¼ cup	cornstarch	50 mL
½ tsp	baking powder	2 mL
¼ tsp	salt	1 mL
1	egg	1
1 cup	water	250 mL
1 tbsp	chopped fresh fennel	15 mL
1 tbsp	chopped fresh basil	15 mL
1 tbsp	chopped fresh thyme	15 mL
1 tbsp	chopped fresh parsley	15 mL
8	scallops	8
8	scampi	8
⅔ lb	fresh cod chopped into 1 inch (2.5 cm) pieces	300 g
	peanut oil for deep-frying	
	fresh basil for garnish	
	radicchio lettuce	
	lemon wedges	

≈ Mix together flour, cornstarch, baking powder and salt. Beat egg and add water; add to flour mixture and mix well. Add fennel, basil, thyme and parsley; mix well and set batter aside.

≈ Preheat oil in deep-fryer to 375°F (190°C).

≈ Coat scallops, scampi and cod in batter and deep-fry in hot oil until golden. Drain well on paper towels. Garnish with basil and serve immediately with radicchio and lemon wedges.

4 SERVINGS

≈≈≈≈≈≈≈≈≈≈≈≈≈≈≈≈≈≈≈

*NOTE: FRITTO MISTO (LITERALLY 'FRIED MIXTURE') IS AN ITALIAN SPECIALTY MADE WITH A VARIETY OF SAVORY FRITTERS.

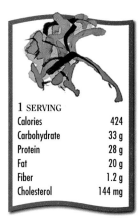

1 SERVING	
Calories	424
Carbohydrate	33 g
Protein	28 g
Fat	20 g
Fiber	1.2 g
Cholesterol	144 mg

SALMON CROQUETTES WITH ALMONDS

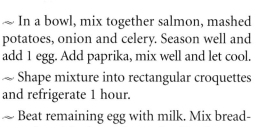

1½ cups	cooked and flaked fresh salmon	375 mL
1½ cups	hot mashed potatoes	375 mL
1	small onion, finely chopped	1
½ cup	finely diced celery	125 mL
2	eggs	2
1	pinch paprika	1
3 tbsp	milk	45 mL
½ cup	breadcrumbs	125 mL
½ cup	almond powder	125 mL
1 cup	all-purpose flour	250 mL
	salt and freshly ground pepper	
	peanut oil for deep-frying	
	mixed greens	
	lime slices	

~ In a bowl, mix together salmon, mashed potatoes, onion and celery. Season well and add 1 egg. Add paprika, mix well and let cool.

~ Shape mixture into rectangular croquettes and refrigerate 1 hour.

~ Beat remaining egg with milk. Mix breadcrumbs with almond powder. Dredge croquettes in flour, dip in egg mixture and coat with breadcrumbs.

~ Preheat oil in deep-fryer to 350°F (180°C). Deep-fry croquettes until golden brown. Drain well on paper towels and serve with mixed greens and slices of lime.

4 SERVINGS

*NOTE: DON'T KEEP ONIONS AND POTATOES TOGETHER. THE ONIONS WILL ABSORB MOISTURE FROM THE POTATOES AND SPOIL.

1 SERVING	
Calories	747
Carbohydrate	54 g
Protein	27 g
Fat	47 g
Fiber	5.0 g
Cholesterol	146 mg

DEEP-FRIED

CALAMARI

2 lbs	fresh squid	1 kg
1 cup	all-purpose flour	250 mL
	juice of 1 lemon	
	salt and freshly ground pepper	
	peanut oil for deep-frying	
	herb mayonnaise (see recipe page 250)	

～ Clean and prepare squid as shown on page 12. Slice into thin rings.

～ Preheat oven to 200°F (100°C). Preheat oil in deep-fryer to 350°F (180°C).

～ Season flour with salt and pepper. Dredge squid rings in flour; shake off any excess. Deep-fry squid, one batch at a time, until golden. Remove with slotted spoon and keep warm in oven. Sprinkle with lemon juice and serve with herb mayonnaise.

4 SERVINGS

*NOTE: THE LARGEST SQUID ON RECORD WAS FOUND OFF THE COAST OF NEWFOUNDLAND IN 1978. IT WAS MORE THAN 50 FEET (16 M) LONG.

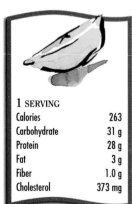

1 SERVING	
Calories	263
Carbohydrate	31 g
Protein	28 g
Fat	3 g
Fiber	1.0 g
Cholesterol	373 mg

*NOTE: WATERCRESS IS ONE OF MANY PLANTS OF THE MUSTARD FAMILY. IT HAS A PEPPERY, SLIGHTLY SPICY TASTE. IF YOU PUT THE STEMS IN A CONTAINER WITH FRESH WATER, AND COVER IT WITH A PLASTIC BAG, IT WILL KEEP FOR UP TO 5 DAYS IN THE REFRIGERATOR.

FRIED SWORDFISH WITH WATERCRESS

1	egg	1
½ cup	milk	125 mL
4	swordfish steaks, about 6 oz (175 g) each	4
½ cup	all-purpose flour	125 mL
1½ cups	breadcrumbs	375 mL
4 cups	fresh watercress	1 L
1 tbsp	olive oil	15 mL
	peanut oil for deep-frying	
	zest of ½ lemon, chopped	
	juice of 1 lemon	
	salt and freshly ground pepper	
	lemon wedges for garnish	

≈ Preheat oil in deep-fryer to 340°F (170°C). Beat egg with milk. Season fish, coat with flour and shake off excess. Dip in egg mixture then dredge in breadcrumbs.

≈ Deep-fry fish in hot oil until golden; remove and drain on paper towels. Sauté watercress in olive oil; add lemon zest and juice. Season with salt and pepper.

≈ Serve swordfish steaks on a bed of watercress, garnished with lemon wedges.

4 SERVINGS

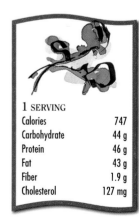

1 SERVING	
Calories	747
Carbohydrate	44 g
Protein	46 g
Fat	43 g
Fiber	1.9 g
Cholesterol	127 mg

$\mathscr{S}$TEAMED

~

Steaming is not only one of the easiest and most

nutritious methods of cooking fish and seafood, but

it ensures that the flesh remains juicy, flavorful and

delicate in texture.

In this chapter, you'll discover a variety of original

recipes that bring together in one pot the fine taste

of fish and seafood, and the flavor and aroma of

fresh herbs and vegetables.

MUSSELS IN CREAMY WHITE WINE SAUCE ≈

6 lbs	fresh mussels, washed, scrubbed and bearded	3 kg
3	dry shallots, finely chopped	3
2 tbsp	chopped fresh parsley	30 mL
2 tbsp	chopped fresh chervil	30 mL
¾ cup	dry white wine	175 mL
2 tbsp	butter	30 mL
½ cup	heavy cream (35% MF)	125 mL
½	red bell pepper, finely chopped	½
	freshly ground pepper	

≈ Place mussels in a large pot. Add shallots, fresh herbs, wine and butter; mix well. Season with pepper, cover and cook over low heat until shells open. Shake pot several times during cooking.

≈ With a slotted spoon, transfer mussels to a bowl, discarding any unopened shells. Continue cooking liquid in pot until reduced by half. Add cream and bring to a boil. Reduce heat to low, add red pepper and mussels, and simmer 3 minutes. Serve immediately.

4 SERVINGS

≈≈≈≈≈≈≈≈≈≈≈≈≈≈≈≈≈≈≈≈≈≈

*NOTE: MUSSELS SHOULD BE EATEN AS SOON AS POSSIBLE AFTER BUYING THEM. COVERED WITH A DAMP CLOTH, THEY WILL KEEP 24 TO 48 HOURS IN THE REFRIGERATOR. THEY WILL DIE IF YOU PUT THEM IN AN AIRTIGHT CONTAINER.

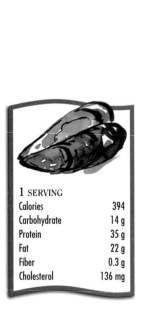

1 SERVING	
Calories	394
Carbohydrate	14 g
Protein	35 g
Fat	22 g
Fiber	0.3 g
Cholesterol	136 mg

Place mussels, shallots, fresh herbs, wine and butter in pot.

Remove cooked mussels with a slotted spoon.

Add cream, then red pepper and mussels to reduced cooking liquid.

PAPRIKA SHRIMP WITH COCKTAIL SAUCE ∼

1½ lbs	fresh medium shrimp	675 g
1 tbsp	paprika	15 mL
	freshly ground pepper	
	Cayenne pepper to taste	
	cocktail sauce (see recipe page 253)	

∼ Peel shrimp, leaving tails intact, and devein. Season with paprika, black pepper and Cayenne pepper.

∼ Place in top part of a large steamer and cover tightly. Steam 5 to 6 minutes, or until they turn pink.

∼ Serve with rice and cocktail sauce.

4 SERVINGS

∼∼∼∼∼∼∼∼∼∼∼∼∼

***NOTE:** SHRIMP ARE LOW IN FAT AND RICH IN VITAMINS AND MINERALS SUCH AS POTASSIUM, PHOSPHOROUS, MAGNESIUM AND IODINE.*

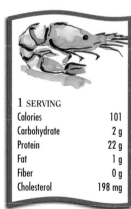

1 SERVING	
Calories	101
Carbohydrate	2 g
Protein	22 g
Fat	1 g
Fiber	0 g
Cholesterol	198 mg

*NOTE: ONIONS WILL KEEP UP TO 2 MONTHS IN A COOL, DRY PLACE. ONCE PEELED, WRAP IN PLASTIC; THEY WILL KEEP 4 DAYS IN THE REFRIGERATOR.

BAY SCALLOPS WITH FRESH TOMATOES AND CHIVES ～

1 tbsp	olive oil	15 mL
1	onion, finely chopped	1
2	garlic cloves, finely chopped	2
6	tomatoes, peeled, seeded and chopped	6
⅓ cup	dry white wine	75 mL
1¼ lbs	fresh small bay scallops	550 g
3 tbsp	chopped fresh chives	45 mL
	salt and freshly ground pepper	
	capellini or any other fresh pasta, cooked al dente	

～ Heat olive oil in frying pan over high heat. Reduce heat, add onion and sauté 3 minutes.

～ Add garlic, tomatoes and wine; season well. Cook 12 minutes over medium heat.

～ Place scallops on top of sauce, season and cook 2 minutes on each side.

～ Sprinkle with fresh chives and serve over cooked pasta.

4 SERVINGS

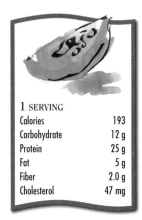

1 SERVING	
Calories	193
Carbohydrate	12 g
Protein	25 g
Fat	5 g
Fiber	2.0 g
Cholesterol	47 mg

*NOTE: UNLIKE ROUND
CABBAGE, WHICH HAS SHINY
LEAVES AND A SHARP TASTE,
NAPA OR CHINESE CABBAGE
HAS THIN, CRISPY LEAVES
WITH A DELICATE FLAVOR.

BONITO WITH CHINESE VEGETABLES

1	1-inch (2.5 cm) piece fresh ginger, peeled and cut in julienne	1
2 tbsp	vegetable oil	30 mL
¼ cup	soy sauce	50 mL
¾ cup	chicken broth	175 mL
1½ lbs	bonito, cut into 8 pieces	675 g
½ lb	Chinese green beans	225 g
3 cups	sliced napa* (Chinese cabbage)	750 mL
3 cups	bean sprouts	750 mL
	salt and freshly ground pepper	

≈ Mix ginger, vegetable oil, soy sauce and chicken broth in a deep dish. Place pieces of bonito in mixture and marinate 1 hour, turning once after 30 minutes.

≈ Steam green beans 3 to 4 minutes in a steam basket. Add napa, bean sprouts and marinated bonito; season well. Cover and steam 7 minutes.

≈ Serve bonito on a bed of vegetables.

4 SERVINGS

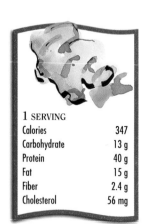

1 SERVING	
Calories	347
Carbohydrate	13 g
Protein	40 g
Fat	15 g
Fiber	2.4 g
Cholesterol	56 mg

RAINBOW TROUT WITH FRESH HERBS

3 tbsp	chopped fresh parsley	45 mL
2 tbsp	chopped fresh chives	30 mL
2 tbsp	chopped fresh basil	30 mL
4	rainbow trout fillets	4
	grated zest of ½ lemon	
	salt and freshly ground pepper	

～ Mix together parsley, chives, basil and lemon zest.

～ Slice each trout fillet in 2 and place in top part of steamer. Season and sprinkle with herb mixture. Steam over low heat about 10 minutes, or until fish is cooked but still moist and juicy.

～ Serve with fresh vegetables, such as asparagus or tomatoes.

4 SERVINGS

*NOTE: THERE ARE TWO MAIN TYPES OF PARSLEY USED IN COOKING: COMMON OR ITALIAN PARSLEY, WITH FLAT, AROMATIC LEAVES; AND CURLY-LEAVED PARSLEY, WHICH IS LESS FLAVORFUL.

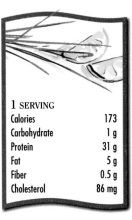

1 SERVING	
Calories	173
Carbohydrate	1 g
Protein	31 g
Fat	5 g
Fiber	0.5 g
Cholesterol	86 mg

Mix together shrimp, mushrooms, chives, soy sauce, sherry, sesame oil, salt and pepper.

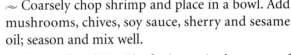

Place 1 tbsp (15 mL) of mixture in the center of each wonton wrapper.

Bring the sides up and press the ends together to make a little purse.

SHRIMP AND MUSHROOM DIM-SUM

½ lb	shrimp, peeled and deveined	225 g
6	mushrooms, finely chopped	6
2 tbsp	finely chopped garlic chives	30 mL
1 tbsp	soy sauce	15 mL
2 tbsp	sherry	30 mL
1 tsp	sesame oil	5 mL
12	wonton wrappers	12
	salt and freshly ground pepper	

≈ Coarsely chop shrimp and place in a bowl. Add mushrooms, chives, soy sauce, sherry and sesame oil; season and mix well.

≈ Place 1 tbsp (15 mL) of mixture in the center of each wonton wrapper. Moisten the ends, bring the sides up and press the ends together to make a little purse.

≈ In a bamboo steamer over boiling water, cook dim-sum 5 minutes over high heat. Serve immediately.

4 SERVINGS

*NOTE: DIM SUM MEANS 'TO PLEASE THE HEART' IN CANTONESE. IN CHINA, THESE LITTLE DUMPLINGS, WHETHER SWEET OR SAVORY, ARE STEAMED OR FRIED AND ARE EATEN IN THE MORNING OR AT NOON WITH TEA.

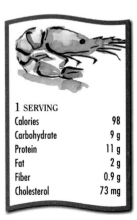

1 SERVING	
Calories	98
Carbohydrate	9 g
Protein	11 g
Fat	2 g
Fiber	0.9 g
Cholesterol	73 mg

CURRIED BLUE CRABS

12	fresh hard shell blue crabs	12
2 tbsp	salt	30 mL
1½ cups	beer	375 mL
½ cup	rice vinegar*	125 mL
1 tbsp	peanut oil	15 mL
1 tbsp	curry powder	15 mL
2 cups	coconut cream	500 mL
3 tbsp	chopped fresh coriander	45 mL
	zest of 1 lime	
	sea salt	

~ Place half the crabs in a large steamer or in the top of a double-boiler. Sprinkle with half the salt. Combine beer and vinegar; pour half of mixture over crabs.

~ Place remaining crabs on top of others in steamer. Add remaining salt and liquid, in that order. Cover and steam 15 to 18 minutes or until they are bright red.

~ Meanwhile, heat oil over medium heat; add curry powder and cook 1 minute. Add coconut cream, lime zest and chopped coriander. Sprinkle with sea salt and cook 10 minutes over medium-low heat. Serve sauce with steamed blue crabs.

4 SERVINGS

~~~~~~~~~~~~~~~~~~~~~~~~~~~~

*NOTE: YOU CAN SUBSTITUTE CIDER OR WINE VINEGAR FOR THE RICE VINEGAR.

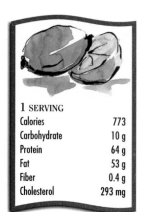

1 SERVING	
Calories	773
Carbohydrate	10 g
Protein	64 g
Fat	53 g
Fiber	0.4 g
Cholesterol	293 mg

CLAMS MARINARA

32	fresh medium clams	32
1 cup	dry white wine	250 mL
2	garlic cloves, chopped	2
2	dry shallots, chopped	2
3 tbsp	butter	45 mL
1 tbsp	chopped fresh thyme	15 mL
1 tbsp	chopped fresh parsley	15 mL
3	tomatoes, seeded and diced	3
	freshly ground pepper	

≈ Wash clams and place in a large saucepan. Add white wine, garlic, shallots and 1 tbsp (15 mL) butter. Cover and cook over medium-high heat until shells open. Shake saucepan several times during cooking.

≈ Remove clams from pan and set aside. Discard any unopened shells. Add remaining butter to cooking liquid and beat with a whisk. Add herbs and tomatoes. Season with pepper and mix well. Add reserved clams and simmer 3 minutes. Serve immediately.

4 SERVINGS

*NOTE: IN MANY RECIPES, CLAMS CAN REPLACE OTHER MOLLUSKS, LIKE OYSTERS AND MUSSELS.

1 SERVING	
Calories	182
Carbohydrate	8 g
Protein	15 g
Fat	10 g
Fiber	0.9 g
Cholesterol	250 mg

*NOTE: FOR A DIFFERENT TASTE, USE WILD MUSHROOMS, LIKE PINE MUSHROOMS OR CHANTERELLES, INSTEAD OF OYSTER MUSHROOMS.

FILLET OF PORGY WITH OYSTER MUSHROOMS

4	porgy fillets, about ⅓ lb (150 g) each	4
1 tbsp	olive oil	15 mL
½ lb	oyster mushrooms	225 g
	salt and freshly ground pepper	
	parsley for garnish	
	lemon slices	

~ Season porgy fillets and place in a bamboo steamer, or on a grill inside a saucepan, above 1 inch (2.5 cm) of water. Cover and cook about 5 minutes over medium heat.

~ Meanwhile, heat olive oil in a sauté pan over high heat, and sauté mushrooms 3 to 4 minutes.

~ Garnish porgy fillets with parsley and lemon slices. Serve with sautéed oyster mushrooms.

4 SERVINGS

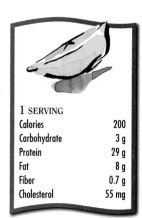

1 SERVING	
Calories	200
Carbohydrate	3 g
Protein	29 g
Fat	8 g
Fiber	0.7 g
Cholesterol	55 mg

STEAMED

RED SNAPPER WITH CAPERS AND OLIVES

2 tbsp	olive oil	30 mL
3	onions, halved and sliced	3
2	garlic cloves, chopped	2
¾ cup	Kalamata olives	175 mL
2 tbsp	capers	30 mL
1 cup	chicken broth	250 mL
2 tbsp	chopped fresh oregano	30 mL
4	small whole red snappers	4
	salt and freshly ground pepper	

≈ Heat oil in a large saucepan; add onions and cook over medium heat about 10 minutes or until lightly browned. Add garlic, olives, capers, chicken broth and oregano. Season and cook about 5 minutes.

≈ Place red snappers (2 at a time, if possible) over onions in saucepan. Cover and cook 5 minutes. Turn fish over and cook about 3 minutes. Remove snappers and keep warm in oven; cook remaining snappers.

≈ When all snappers are done, serve over bed of onion, caper and olive sauce.

4 SERVINGS

*NOTE: CAPERS CAN BE FOUND PICKLED IN VINEGAR OR PRESERVED IN BRINE. THE LATTER SHOULD BE THOROUGHLY RINSED BEFORE THEY ARE USED.

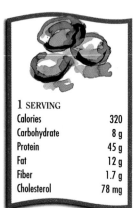

1 SERVING	
Calories	320
Carbohydrate	8 g
Protein	45 g
Fat	12 g
Fiber	1.7 g
Cholesterol	78 mg

*NOTE: ORANGES WILL KEEP FOR A FEW DAYS AT ROOM TEMPERATURE OR MORE THAN 2 WEEKS IN THE REFRIGERATOR.

MUSSELS WITH ORANGE-CORIANDER SAUCE

4 lbs	mussels, washed, scrubbed and bearded	2 kg
½ cup	orange juice	125 mL
¼ cup	lime juice	50 mL
2 tbsp	fish sauce (nam pla)	30 mL
½ cup	dry white wine	125 mL
1 tbsp	coriander seeds, crushed	15 mL
2	garlic cloves, chopped	2
	zest of ½ orange	
	freshly ground pepper	

～ Place all ingredients in a large saucepan and season with pepper. Cover and cook over high heat until shells open. Shake saucepan several times during cooking. Discard any unopened mussels.

～ Serve mussels with sauce.

4 SERVINGS

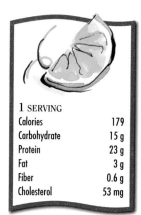

1 SERVING	
Calories	179
Carbohydrate	15 g
Protein	23 g
Fat	3 g
Fiber	0.6 g
Cholesterol	53 mg

SALMON AND GOAT CHEESE ROLLS WITH BEURRE BLANC

24	large spinach leaves	24
1 tbsp	olive oil	15 mL
1	leek, white part only, diced	1
1 tbsp	chopped fresh rosemary	15 mL
½ lb	goat cheese	225 g
4	slices salmon fillet, about ⅓ lb (150 g) each, skinned	4
1 cup	beurre blanc* (see recipe page 252)	250 mL
2 tbsp	chopped fresh chives	30 mL
	salt and freshly ground pepper	

∼ Preheat oven to 350°F (180°C).

∼ Blanch spinach in boiling, salted water. Drain well and set aside.

∼ In a sauté pan, heat oil over medium heat; sauté leek 3 minutes. Add rosemary, season and continue cooking 1 minute. Remove from heat and add goat cheese; mix well.

∼ With a knife, slice each piece of salmon open (making the salmon half as thick), leaving an inch (2.5 cm) intact at one end; lay it out on top of the spinach leaves. Spread the goat cheese filling inside the salmon and close it up again. Season well, cover with spinach leaves, and wrap it in plastic.

∼ Place salmon on a grill, and then the grill in a baking dish. Pour 1 inch (2.5 cm) of water in the baking dish and cover with aluminum foil. The fish should not touch the water. Cook in oven about 20 minutes.

∼ Let stand 5 minutes and serve with beurre blanc and chives.

4 SERVINGS

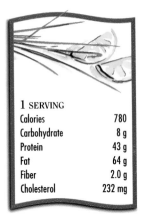

1 SERVING	
Calories	780
Carbohydrate	8 g
Protein	43 g
Fat	64 g
Fiber	2.0 g
Cholesterol	232 mg

Sauté leek in hot olive oil and add rosemary.

Stir in goat cheese.

Slice the salmon open (making the salmon half as thick), leaving an inch (2.5 cm) intact at one end.

*NOTE: TOO HIGH A
TEMPERATURE WILL TURN
THE BEURRE BLANC.
PREPARE IT OVER LOW HEAT,
OR IN A DOUBLE-BOILER.

Lay salmon out over spinach leaves.

Spread the goat cheese filling inside the salmon and close it up again.

Cover and wrap with spinach leaves.

STEAMED

*NOTE: DO NOT MISTAKE THE JUICE OF A COCONUT WITH COCONUT MILK, WHICH IS MADE FROM THE GRATED PULP OF THE COCONUT. THE PULP IS PURÉED, THEN MIXED WITH HOT WATER OR MILK. COCONUT MILK IS SOLD IN CANS.

THAI SEAFOOD TERRINES ≈

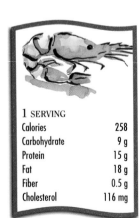

1 SERVING	
Calories	258
Carbohydrate	9 g
Protein	15 g
Fat	18 g
Fiber	0.5 g
Cholesterol	116 mg

⅓ lb	white fish fillets, finely chopped	150 g
⅓ lb	fresh shrimp, peeled, deveined and finely chopped	150 g
2 tbsp	fish sauce (nam pla)	30 mL
1¼ cups	coconut milk*	300 mL
¼ cup	chopped fresh Thai basil	50 mL
1 tbsp	chopped lime zest	15 mL
2	garlic cloves, chopped	2
1	red chili pepper, seeded and finely chopped	1
1	egg, beaten	1
2 tbsp	rice flour	30 mL

≈ Preheat oven to 400°F (200°C).

≈ Combine fish and shrimp. Add fish sauce, coconut milk, basil, lime zest, garlic and chili pepper. Marinate 30 minutes. Add egg and rice flour; mix well.

≈ Transfer to 4 individual ramekins and place in a baking dish or roasting pan with 1 inch (2.5 cm) of water in the bottom. Cook in oven about 25 minutes. Serve immediately.

4 SERVINGS

116

PORGIES WITH FENNEL

1	fennel bulb, sliced	1
1	red bell pepper, sliced	1
2	leeks, white part only, sliced	2
2	fresh parsley sprigs	2
4	porgies, about ¾ lb (350 g) each	4
	salt and freshly ground pepper	

≈ Place fennel, red pepper and leek in a steamer above 1 inch (2.5 cm) of water. Add parsley and place seasoned porgies on top.

≈ Cover and cook over low heat 15 minutes, or until fish is opaque and slightly firm.

≈ Serve fish on the bed of vegetables, with steamed new potatoes, if desired.

4 SERVINGS

*NOTE: FENNEL IS RICH IN VITAMIN A. IT ALSO CONTAINS CALCIUM, PHOSPHOROUS AND POTASSIUM. IT WILL KEEP MORE THAN 5 DAYS IN A PLASTIC BAG IN THE REFRIGERATOR.

1 SERVING	
Calories	295
Carbohydrate	10 g
Protein	48 g
Fat	7 g
Fiber	1.5 g
Cholesterol	78 mg

$\mathcal{P}$OACHED

~

Poaching is an excellent way to cook all kinds of fish

and seafood. Not only is it quick and easy, but by

gently simmering the fish in liquids such as wine, fish

stock or milk, you are sure to preserve the full flavor

and texture of these delicate foods.

This chapter offers both traditional favorites and

original recipes from around the world, from

Poached Boston Bluefish *to* Fresh Cod à la

Dijonnaise. *The difficulty lies in choosing!*

GROUPER POT-AU-FEU

2 tbsp	butter	30 mL
4	thick grouper steaks	4
2	garlic cloves, chopped	2
4	small onions	4
4	whole cloves	4
2	fresh parsley sprigs	2
2	bay leaves	2
4 cups	chicken or vegetable broth	1 L
3	carrots, cut in 1-inch (2.5 cm) pieces	3
3	parsnips, cut in 1-inch (2.5 cm) pieces	3
2	corn cobs, cut in 2-inch (5 cm) pieces	2
	salt and freshly ground pepper	

~ In a large saucepan, melt butter over medium heat; season grouper steaks and sauté 1 minute on each side.

~ Add garlic, onions studded with cloves, parsley, bay leaves and broth. Cook 5 minutes.

~ Add carrots, parsnips and corn. Continue cooking 10 minutes or until fish is cooked. Correct seasoning and serve very hot.

4 SERVINGS

*NOTE: CORN ON THE COB SHOULD BE EATEN THE SAME DAY IT IS PICKED BECAUSE ITS NATURAL SUGARS ARE THEN CONVERTED TO STARCH.

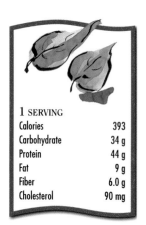

1 SERVING	
Calories	393
Carbohydrate	34 g
Protein	44 g
Fat	9 g
Fiber	6.0 g
Cholesterol	90 mg

FRESH COD À LA DIJONNAISE

2 cups	fish stock	500 mL
1½ lbs	fresh cod fillets	675 g
3 tbsp	butter	45 mL
3 tbsp	all-purpose flour	45 mL
2 tbsp	Dijon mustard	30 mL
2 tbsp	chopped fresh tarragon	
	salt and freshly ground pepper	

~ In a saucepan, bring fish stock to a boil. Reduce heat to low and poach cod fillets 5 minutes in lightly simmering stock. Remove fillets with a slotted spoon and keep warm.

~ In another saucepan, melt butter. Add flour and hot fish stock; bring to a boil. Reduce heat and stir in mustard and tarragon; correct seasoning. Serve fish topped with sauce. Accompany with asparagus, if desired.

4 SERVINGS

*NOTE: DIJON MUSTARD IS PRODUCED WITH VERJUICE AND WHITE WINE. THE TERM 'À LA DIJONNAISE' REFERS TO DISHES PREPARED WITH A SPECIALTY OF DIJON, FRANCE, PARTICULARLY MUSTARD (FOR SAVORY DISHES) OR BLACKCURRANTS (FOR SWEET DISHES).

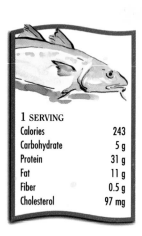

1 SERVING	
Calories	243
Carbohydrate	5 g
Protein	31 g
Fat	11 g
Fiber	0.5 g
Cholesterol	97 mg

~~~~~~~~~~~~~~~~~~

*NOTE: STRIPED BASS
NORMALLY HAS LONG,
STRAIGHT STRIPES. BUT THE
STRIPES ON FARMED STRIPED
BASS ARE FRAGMENTED AND
IRREGULAR.

STRIPED BASS WITH CORIANDER AND TOMATOES ~

½ cup	dry white wine	125 mL
½ cup	fish stock	125 mL
4	striped bass fillets	4
1	garlic clove, chopped	1
6	tomatoes, peeled, seeded and chopped	6
¼ cup	chopped fresh coriander	50 mL
	lime juice	
	lime slices for garnish	
	salt and freshly ground pepper	

~ In a saucepan, bring the white wine and fish stock to a boil. Reduce heat to medium; add bass fillets and poach 7 minutes. Remove with a slotted spoon and set aside.

~ Bring broth back to a boil; add garlic and tomatoes. Season well. Reduce heat to medium and let simmer 10 minutes. Add coriander and mix well.

~ Return fillets to pan and reheat 3 minutes. Sprinkle each fillet with lime juice, garnish with lime slices and serve with sauce.

4 SERVINGS

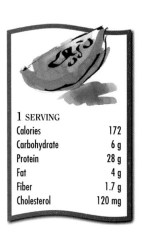

1 SERVING	
Calories	172
Carbohydrate	6 g
Protein	28 g
Fat	4 g
Fiber	1.7 g
Cholesterol	120 mg

TURBOT FILLETS IN SAFFRON BROTH

4	small turbot fillets, about 2½ oz (75 g) each	4
2	dry shallots, chopped	2
½ lb	mushrooms, diced	225 g
1½ cups	dry white wine	375 mL
1 cup	fish stock	250 mL
1	pinch saffron	1
2	small zucchini, thinly sliced	2
	fresh chives for garnish	
	salt and freshly ground pepper	

≈ Place turbot fillets in frying pan. Add shallots, mushrooms, wine, fish stock and saffron; season well. Cover and bring to a boil over medium heat. Turn fish over, reduce heat to low and simmer 2 minutes. Remove fish from pan and keep warm.

≈ Add zucchini to hot broth and cook 1 minute. To serve, arrange zucchini slices around the contour of each plate, place fillet in the center and top with hot saffron broth. Sprinkle with fresh chives.

4 SERVINGS

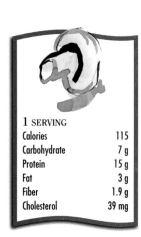

1 SERVING	
Calories	115
Carbohydrate	7 g
Protein	15 g
Fat	3 g
Fiber	1.9 g
Cholesterol	39 mg

Add mushrooms to fish in frying pan.

Remove cooked fish and keep warm.

Add zucchini to hot broth and cook 1 minute.

~~~~~~~~~~

*NOTE: TODAY, SAFFRON IS GROWN MAINLY IN SPAIN, IRAN AND SOUTH AMERICA. IT IS VERY EXPENSIVE BECAUSE IT TAKES AT LEAST 60,000 DRIED FLOWERS OF THE PLANT TO MAKE 1 LB (450 G) OF SAFFRON SPICE.

Arrange zucchini slices around the contour of each plate.

Place fillet in the center.

Top with hot saffron broth.

PIKE QUENELLES WITH LOBSTER BISQUE

1 cup	water	250 mL
3 tbsp	butter	45 mL
1¼ cups	all-purpose flour	300 mL
½ tsp	salt	2 mL
1	egg	1
1 lb	pike flesh	450 g
6	egg whites	6
2 cups	heavy cream (35% MF)	500 mL
4 tbsp	softened butter	60 mL
2 cups	fish stock or water	500 mL
	grated nutmeg to taste	
	salt and freshly ground pepper	
	lobster bisque (see recipe page 50)	

∼ Place water and butter in a saucepan and bring to a boil. Add flour and salt; stir until mixture comes away from sides of pan. Remove from heat, add egg and mix well. Set aside.

∼ In a food processor, purée the pike flesh. Add egg whites, one at a time, blending after each addition. Add half of cream and blend until smooth. Add batter and nutmeg; season and mix well.

∼ Strain mixture through a sieve; add softened butter and remaining cream. Refrigerate 30 minutes. Meanwhile, bring the fish stock to a boil and reduce heat.

∼ With 2 wet spoons, shape the fish mixture into quenelles and poach in simmering stock about 15 minutes. Serve hot with lobster bisque, if desired.

4 SERVINGS

*NOTE: QUENELLES ARE SERVED AS AN ENTRÉE WITH A SAUCE, AU GRATIN OR SOMETIMES AS A GARNISH FOR SOUPS. THE WORD COMES FROM THE GERMAN WORD KNÖDEL (DUMPLING).

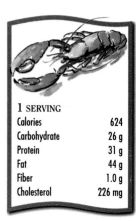

1 SERVING	
Calories	624
Carbohydrate	26 g
Protein	31 g
Fat	44 g
Fiber	1.0 g
Cholesterol	226 mg

*NOTE: TO KEEP ASPARAGUS
FRESH AND TENDER, PLACE
STALKS IN A CONTAINER WITH
WATER, COVER WITH A PLASTIC
BAG AND REFRIGERATE.

POACHED HALIBUT WITH FRESH VEGETABLES

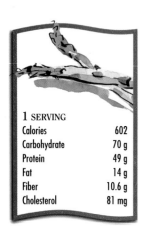

1 SERVING	
Calories	602
Carbohydrate	70 g
Protein	49 g
Fat	14 g
Fiber	10.6 g
Cholesterol	81 mg

2	dry shallots, chopped	2
½ cup	dry white wine	125 mL
4 cups	fish stock	1 L
4	halibut steaks, about 6 oz (175 g) each	4
3 tbsp	butter	45 mL
1 tbsp	chopped fresh parsley	15 mL
12	fresh asparagus	12
4	green onions	4
8	spring carrots	8
12	small red potatoes	12
	salt and freshly ground pepper	

≈ Place shallots, wine and fish stock in a saucepan. Season well, cover and bring to a boil. Reduce heat to medium, season halibut steaks and poach in the saucepan 8 to 10 minutes, or adjust time depending on size.

≈ When fish is cooked, remove from saucepan and keep warm.

≈ Bring broth back to a boil; add butter and parsley. Cook each vegetable separately about 4 minutes in broth, or until tender but still *al dente*.

≈ Serve halibut steaks with vegetables and broth.

4 SERVINGS

POACHED SALMON WITH VEGETABLE JULIENNE ～

3 cups	fish stock	750 mL
4	salmon steaks	4
1	small zucchini, cut in julienne	1
1	yellow bell pepper, cut in julienne	1
1	red bell pepper, cut in julienne	1
2 tbsp	butter	30 mL
1 tbsp	chopped fresh parsley	15 mL
	juice of ½ lemon	
	salt and freshly ground pepper	

～ Bring fish stock to a boil in saucepan over high heat. Reduce heat to low, add salmon and cook 15 minutes. When cooked, remove salmon with a slotted spoon and set aside.

～ Heat stock over high heat. Add vegetable julienne and cook 1 minute. Add butter, lemon juice and chopped parsley; correct seasoning.

～ Pour sauce and vegetables in a shallow dish, place fish on top and serve. Accompany with fresh pasta, if desired.

4 SERVINGS

*NOTE: CHOOSE SMALL ZUCCHINI IF POSSIBLE; THE SMALLER THEY ARE, THE MORE FLAVORFUL.

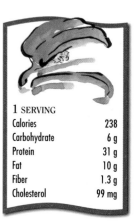

1 SERVING	
Calories	238
Carbohydrate	6 g
Protein	31 g
Fat	10 g
Fiber	1.3 g
Cholesterol	99 mg

LOBSTER AND HADDOCK WITH TARRAGON SAUCE

2 tbsp	butter	30 mL
3	dry shallots, sliced	3
⅓ cup	dry white wine	75 mL
1 cup	fish stock	250 mL
4	haddock fillets, about ¼ lb (115 g) each	4
8	small lobster tails, cooked	8
2 tbsp	chopped fresh tarragon	30 mL
	salt and freshly ground pepper	

∼ Melt butter in a medium saucepan and sauté shallots 2 minutes.

∼ Add wine and fish stock; bring to a boil. Reduce heat to medium-low and add haddock; season, cover and cook 5 minutes. Remove fillets with a slotted spoon and keep warm.

∼ Reduce heat to low. Reheat lobster tails in fish stock 3 minutes. Add tarragon and let simmer 3 minutes.

∼ Arrange 1 haddock fillet and 2 lobster tails on each plate. Drizzle with tarragon sauce and serve with fresh vegetables and pasta, if desired.

4 SERVINGS

*NOTE: THERE ARE TWO KINDS OF TARRAGON. THE TOOTHED GREEN LEAVES HAVE A FINE, DELICATE FLAVOR AND ARE USED TO SEASON SALADS AND SOUPS; WHEN COOKED, THEY ARE USED TO FLAVOR AND GARNISH DIFFERENT DISHES. RUSSIAN TARRAGON IS LIGHTER IN COLOR AND MORE BITTER TASTING.

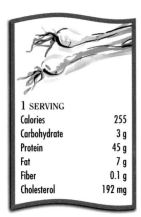

1 SERVING	
Calories	255
Carbohydrate	3 g
Protein	45 g
Fat	7 g
Fiber	0.1 g
Cholesterol	192 mg

SALTED COD À LA CRÉOLE

1 lb	boneless salted cod	450 g
2 tbsp	olive oil	30 mL
2	onions, chopped	2
1	red bell pepper, diced	1
1	green bell pepper, diced	1
2	garlic cloves, chopped	2
½ cup	dry white wine	125 mL
5	large tomatoes, peeled, seeded and chopped	5
1 tbsp	chopped fresh thyme	15 mL
2 tbsp	chopped fresh parsley	30 mL
	freshly ground pepper	

~ Place salted cod in a big bowl of cold water and soak 8 hours. Rinse and change water twice during soaking. Drain cod and transfer to saucepan. Cover with cold water and bring to a boil. Rinse cod and set aside.

~ Heat oil in frying pan over medium heat. Reduce heat to low, add onions and cook 4 minutes. Add red pepper, green pepper and garlic; cook 4 minutes. Add wine and tomatoes; continue cooking 10 minutes.

~ Break cod into big chunks and return to saucepan with sauce; cook 10 minutes. Add thyme and parsley; mix well. Correct seasoning and serve over hot rice.

4 SERVINGS

*NOTE: TO PEEL TOMATOES, REMOVE THE CORE AND CUT AN X INTO THE SKIN ON THE OTHER SIDE. PLACE IN BOILING WATER 1 TO 2 MINUTES, AND PEEL, STARTING FROM THE X.

1 SERVING	
Calories	216
Carbohydrate	11 g
Protein	25 g
Fat	8 g
Fiber	2.6 g
Cholesterol	57 mg

~~~~~~~~~~~~~~~

*NOTE: CELERY STALKS
SHOULD BE FIRM AND BRIGHT
GREEN. SEPARATE STALKS
AND KEEP IN A PLASTIC BAG
IN THE REFRIGERATOR.

POACHED BOSTON BLUEFISH

1 tbsp	butter	15 mL
2	carrots, peeled and sliced	2
2	leeks, white part only, sliced	2
2	celery stalks, sliced	2
3 cups	fish stock	750 mL
¼ tsp	fennel seeds	1 mL
1 lb	Boston bluefish fillets	450 g
	juice of ½ lemon	
	sea salt and freshly ground pepper	

~ Heat butter in sauté pan over medium heat. Add vegetables and cook 3 minutes. Add fish stock, fennel seeds and seasonings; bring to a boil. Reduce heat to medium-low and cook, uncovered, 10 minutes.

~ Place fillets in broth, add lemon juice and cook 4 to 5 minutes over low heat. Carefully remove fillets and serve with vegetables and broth.

4 SERVINGS

1 SERVING	
Calories	224
Carbohydrate	14 g
Protein	24 g
Fat	8 g
Fiber	2.4 g
Cholesterol	75 mg

133

WHOLE POACHED BABY SALMON

1	bay leaf	1
6	fresh parsley sprigs	6
6	fresh dill sprigs	6
6	fresh thyme sprigs	6
2 tbsp	chopped fresh chives	30 mL
2	carrots, sliced	2
2	leeks, white part only, sliced	2
1 cup	dry white wine	250 mL
1 cup	water	250 mL
1	4 lb (2 kg) baby salmon	1
	salt and freshly ground pepper	
	juice of 1 lemon	
	lemon slices	
	dill sprigs for garnish	

≈ Place herbs, vegetables, wine and water in large saucepan. Season and cook 15 minutes over low heat.

≈ Transfer contents to a fish kettle (poacher).* Place fish on rack inside kettle. Add enough water to cover salmon and sprinkle with lemon juice. Place kettle on stove over low heat, cover and cook about 20 minutes or until fish flesh is firm and almost opaque. Do not boil.

≈ Serve salmon with lemon slices and steamed new potatoes, if desired. Garnish with sprigs of dill.

4 SERVINGS

≈≈≈≈≈≈≈≈≈≈≈≈≈≈≈≈≈

*NOTE: INSTEAD OF A FISH KETTLE, YOU CAN USE A RELATIVELY DEEP BAKING DISH THAT IS LARGE ENOUGH TO HOLD THE WHOLE FISH.

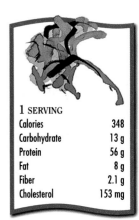

1 SERVING	
Calories	348
Carbohydrate	13 g
Protein	56 g
Fat	8 g
Fiber	2.1 g
Cholesterol	153 mg

POACHED LOBSTER WITH LEMON GARLIC BUTTER ～

4	live lobsters, 1¼ lbs (550 g) each	4
1 cup	butter	250 mL
2	garlic cloves, finely chopped	2
2 tbsp	chopped fresh parsley	30 mL
	lemon juice	

～ Plunge lobsters into stockpot filled with boiling water. Cook 12 to 14 minutes over medium heat; do not let water resume full boil.

～ As soon as lobsters are cooked, remove from pot and drain well.

～ Melt butter in small saucepan; add garlic, parsley and lemon juice to taste. Serve lobster with garlic butter and steamed rice, if desired.

4 SERVINGS

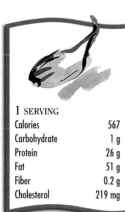

1 SERVING	
Calories	567
Carbohydrate	1 g
Protein	26 g
Fat	51 g
Fiber	0.2 g
Cholesterol	219 mg

SKATE WITH CAPER BUTTER

1½ lb	skate, cleaned	675 g
2 tbsp	white wine vinegar	30 mL
1	carrot, sliced	1
2	dry shallots, chopped	2
¼ cup	butter	50 mL
2 tbsp	capers	30 mL
2 tbsp	chopped fresh parsley	30 mL
	juice of ½ lemon	
	salt and freshly ground pepper	

≈ Place skate in a saucepan. Cover with water and add vinegar, carrot and shallots; season well. Bring to a boil, reduce heat to low and cook 15 minutes.

≈ Remove fish with a slotted spoon, drain well and set aside on heated serving platter; keep warm.

≈ Melt butter in a frying pan over high heat. Add capers, parsley and lemon juice; mix well. Pour over fish and serve with sautéed potatoes.

4 SERVINGS

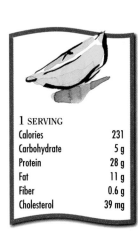

1 SERVING	
Calories	231
Carbohydrate	5 g
Protein	28 g
Fat	11 g
Fiber	0.6 g
Cholesterol	39 mg

137

*NOTE: A BOUQUET GARNI IS A SELECTION OF AROMATIC PLANTS TIED TOGETHER, USUALLY IN A CHEESECLOTH. IT IS GENERALLY MADE WITH 3 SPRIGS OF PARSLEY, 1 SPRIG OF THYME AND 1 OR 2 BAY LEAVES. IT CAN ALSO INCLUDE SAVORY, SAGE, ROSEMARY, CELERY OR OTHER FINE HERBS.

Add bouquet garni to fish stock.

Place fish pieces in stock.

Remove cooked fish with a slotted spoon.

PORGY À LA NAGE

4 cups	fish stock	1 L
1	bouquet garni*	1
1 tsp	fennel seeds	5 mL
1	whole porgy, cut in sections	1
1 lb	rutabagas, peeled and cubed	450 g
½ lb	green beans, pared and tied in bunches	225 g
½	Savoy cabbage, sliced in 8 pieces	½
2 tbsp	butter	30 mL
	salt and freshly ground pepper	

∼ In a stewpot, bring fish stock to a boil. Reduce heat to medium, add bouquet garni and fennel seeds; cook 5 minutes.

∼ Place pieces of porgy in stewpot, season and cook 7 to 8 minutes. Remove with slotted spoon and set aside.

∼ Bring stock to a boil, add rutabaga and cook 10 minutes. Add green beans and cabbage; continue cooking 5 minutes.

∼ Add butter and return fish to pot; reheat 5 minutes. Serve very hot.

4 SERVINGS

1 SERVING	
Calories	204
Carbohydrate	18 g
Protein	15 g
Fat	8 g
Fiber	5.0 g
Cholesterol	35 mg

Cook rutabaga in stock.

Add green beans and cabbage.

Return fish to pot and reheat 5 minutes.

EEL MATELOTE

4 tbsp	butter	60 mL
1¾ lbs	eel, cut in sections	800 g
2	onions, sliced	2
4 tbsp	cognac	60 mL
1½ cups	red wine	375 mL
2	fresh parsley sprigs	2
2	fresh thyme sprigs	2
1	bay leaf	1
2	garlic cloves, chopped	2
2 tbsp	all-purpose flour	30 mL
1 cup	pearl onions	250 mL
½ lb	mushroom caps	225 g
½ cup	diced salt pork, blanched	125 mL
3 tbsp	chopped fresh parsley	45 mL

≈ Melt 2 tbsp (30 mL) of butter in a stewpot over medium heat. Add eel pieces and onions and sauté 3 minutes. Pour in cognac and bring to a boil.

≈ Add red wine and enough water to cover the eel pieces. Add parsley, thyme, bay leaf and garlic; simmer 20 minutes over low heat. Remove eel pieces and keep warm.

≈ Bring cooking liquid to a boil. Combine 2 tbsp (30 mL) softened butter with flour and add this mixture, little by little, to broth, stirring constantly.

≈ In a frying pan, sauté pearl onions, mushrooms and salt pork in a little butter; add to sauce. Return eel pieces to stewpot and add chopped parsley. Serve hot with boiled potatoes.

4 SERVINGS

≈≈≈≈≈≈≈≈≈≈≈≈≈≈≈≈≈≈≈≈≈≈

*NOTE: MATELOTE IS A FISH STEW MADE WITH RED OR WHITE WINE AND AROMATIC FLAVORINGS. IT IS USUALLY MADE WITH EEL, BUT CAN ALSO BE MADE WITH CARP, TROUT OR OTHER TYPES OF FRESHWATER FISH.

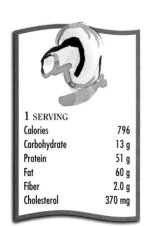

1 SERVING	
Calories	796
Carbohydrate	13 g
Protein	51 g
Fat	60 g
Fiber	2.0 g
Cholesterol	370 mg

SAUTÉED

~

Nothing quite compares to the simplicity and delight

of sautéed fish and seafood. Golden all over, slightly

crispy on the outside and soft on the inside, who can

resist the temptation?

This chapter offers some of the simplest yet most

tantalizing combinations. From Dover Sole with

Shallots and Orange *to* Scallops in Pernod Sauce,

there is no limit to the mouth-watering dishes

you can prepare in minutes.

RED SNAPPER WITH MARINATED PEPPERS

2	large yellow bell peppers	2
2	large red bell peppers	2
2 tbsp	olive oil	30 mL
2 tbsp	extra virgin olive oil	30 mL
2	garlic cloves, finely chopped	2
1 tbsp	balsamic vinegar	15 mL
4	red snapper fillets, unskinned	4
	sea salt and freshly ground pepper	

~ Preheat oven to 400°F (200°C). Slit bell peppers in half and place, cut-side-down, in roasting pan. Brush with 1 tbsp (15 mL) olive oil. Cook 15 to 20 minutes in oven, or until skin is lightly browned.

~ Place bell peppers in a bowl, cover with plastic wrap and let cool 20 minutes. Skin peppers and remove membranes and seeds. Slice each half pepper into 4 and place in a bowl. Add extra virgin olive oil, garlic and balsamic vinegar. Season and marinate at least 1 hour.

~ Season fish. In a large frying pan, heat remaining 1 tbsp (15 mL) olive oil over medium-high heat. Add fish and cook 3 minutes on each side or until flesh is firm. Serve over marinated peppers.

4 SERVINGS

*NOTE: IN AN AIRTIGHT CONTAINER AWAY FROM DIRECT SUNLIGHT, PEPPERCORNS WILL KEEP INDEFINITELY. BUT GROUND PEPPER QUICKLY LOSES ITS FLAVOR AND AROMA.

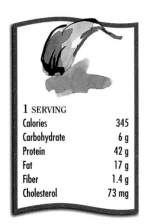

1 SERVING	
Calories	345
Carbohydrate	6 g
Protein	42 g
Fat	17 g
Fiber	1.4 g
Cholesterol	73 mg

SCALLOPS IN PERNOD SAUCE

3 tbsp	butter	45 mL
2	dry shallots, chopped	2
1¼ lbs	fresh scallops	550 g
4 tbsp	Pernod (anise liqueur)	60 mL
¼ tsp	fennel seeds	1 mL
1 tbsp	chopped fresh chervil	15 mL
1 cup	fish stock	250 mL
¼ cup	heavy cream (35% MF)	50 mL
	chopped fresh parsley	
	salt and freshly ground pepper	

≈ Heat butter in frying pan over high heat. Add shallots and cook 2 minutes. Add scallops and cook 1 minute on each side.

≈ Pour in Pernod and flambé. As soon as the flames die out, remove scallops and set aside. Add fennel seeds, chopped chervil and fish stock; season and cook 2 minutes over high heat. Reduce heat, add cream and simmer 2 minutes.

≈ Return scallops to frying pan, sprinkle with fresh parsley and simmer 2 minutes. Serve with green beans, if desired.

4 SERVINGS

*NOTE: SCALLOPS ARE COOKED WHEN THEY ARE OPAQUE, WITH ONLY THE CENTER REMAINING SLIGHTLY TRANSPARENT. THEY WILL HARDEN IF OVERCOOKED.

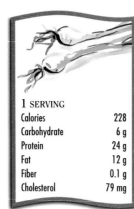

1 SERVING	
Calories	228
Carbohydrate	6 g
Protein	24 g
Fat	12 g
Fiber	0.1 g
Cholesterol	79 mg

*NOTE: RICE VINEGAR IS MADE FROM RICE WINE THAT HAS BEEN ACETIFIED AND FERMENTED. JAPANESE RICE VINEGAR IS CLEAR AND RELATIVELY SWEET COMPARED TO THE MORE ACIDIC, CHINESE VARIETY.

HADDOCK WITH NUOC CHAM SAUCE

4 tbsp	nuoc-mam (fish sauce)	60 mL
4	dry shallots, sliced	4
3	garlic cloves, chopped	3
1	red chili pepper, finely chopped	1
2 tbsp	brown sugar	30 mL
2 tbsp	rice vinegar	30 mL
4	tomatoes, peeled, seeded and diced	4
2 tbsp	peanut oil	30 mL
4	haddock fillets, about 6 oz (175 g) each	4
2	zucchini, in sticks	2
	juice of 1 lime	
	sea salt	

~ In a blender, combine nuoc-mam sauce, shallots, garlic, red chili pepper, brown sugar, rice vinegar and lime juice. Blend until puréed.

~ Transfer purée to saucepan; add tomatoes, season well and cook 10 minutes over medium-low heat.

~ Heat peanut oil in a frying pan over medium-high heat. Add haddock fillets, season and cook 2 minutes on each side. Serve fillets with sauce and sautéed zucchini.

4 SERVINGS

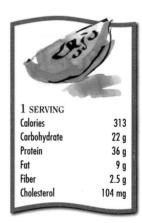

1 SERVING	
Calories	313
Carbohydrate	22 g
Protein	36 g
Fat	9 g
Fiber	2.5 g
Cholesterol	104 mg

STIR-FRIED SHRIMP WITH BOK-CHOY

1 lb	large shrimp, peeled and deveined	450 g
2 tbsp	sherry	30 mL
3 tbsp	soy sauce	45 mL
2 tbsp	finely chopped fresh ginger	30 mL
4	green onions, chopped	4
3	garlic cloves, chopped	3
3 tbsp	peanut oil	45 mL
15	shiitake mushrooms, sliced	15
1	head bok-choy (Chinese cabbage), coarsely chopped	1
2	red bell peppers, cubed	2
¼ tsp	chili paste	1 mL

~ In large bowl, place shrimp, sherry, soy sauce, ginger, onions and garlic. Toss well and marinate 30 minutes.

~ Heat 2 tbsp (30 mL) peanut oil in a wok over high heat.* Drain shrimp, reserving marinade, and stir-fry 2 minutes; remove and set aside. Add remaining oil to wok. Add shiitake mushrooms and cook 2 minutes. Add bok-choy and red pepper; continue cooking 4 to 5 minutes.

~ Stir chili paste into reserved marinade; pour into wok and simmer 2 minutes. Return shrimp to wok, mix well and simmer 2 more minutes. Serve with steamed rice.

4 SERVINGS

*NOTE: HEAT THE WOK, THEN POUR IN PEANUT OIL AND WAIT UNTIL OIL IS HOT BEFORE STIR-FRYING THE INGREDIENTS. IF THE OIL IS NOT HOT ENOUGH, THE INGREDIENTS WILL STICK TO THE WOK.

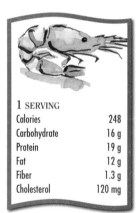

1 SERVING	
Calories	248
Carbohydrate	16 g
Protein	19 g
Fat	12 g
Fiber	1.3 g
Cholesterol	120 mg

SALMON TROUT FILLETS WITH ASPARAGUS PURÉE ~

1	bunch fresh asparagus, diced	1
2 tbsp	extra virgin olive oil	30 mL
1 tbsp	olive oil	15 mL
4	salmon trout fillets, about 6 oz (175 g) each, skinned	4
	juice of ½ lemon	
	fresh chives	
	small patty pan squash	
	salt and freshly ground pepper	

Remove cooked asparagus with a slotted spoon, reserving ½ cup (125 mL) of cooking liquid.

~ Cook asparagus in salted boiling water 4 minutes. Drain, reserving ½ cup (125 mL) cooking liquid. Place asparagus and reserved liquid in blender and blend until smooth. Gradually add extra virgin olive oil, blending well after each addition. Strain purée through a sieve and set aside.

~ Heat olive oil in large frying pan over medium-high heat. Season fillets and cook 2 minutes on each side.

~ Sprinkle fillets with lemon juice. Spoon asparagus purée among 4 individual plates and place fillets on top. Garnish with fresh chives and patty pan squash.

4 SERVINGS

Purée in blender; gradually add extra virgin olive oil, blending well after each addition.

~~~~~~~~~~~~~~~~~~~~~~~~~~~~

*NOTE: NON-REFINED EXTRA VIRGIN OLIVE OIL IS THE PRODUCT OF THE FIRST COLD PRESSING OF OLIVES. THE FLAVOR, COLOR AND AROMA ARE PURE WITH LESS THAN 1% ACIDITY.

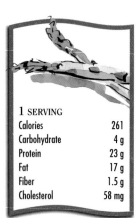

1 SERVING	
Calories	261
Carbohydrate	4 g
Protein	23 g
Fat	17 g
Fiber	1.5 g
Cholesterol	58 mg

Strain purée through a sieve and set aside.

SAUTÉED

151

*NOTE: To keep them as fresh as possible, mushrooms should be placed in a brown paper bag in the refrigerator.

TUNA WITH MUSHROOMS AND HERB BUTTER

3 tbsp	olive oil	45 mL
4	tuna steaks, about 6 oz (175 g) each	4
5 oz	fresh portabella mushrooms, sliced	150 g
7 oz	fresh oyster mushrooms	200 g
4 tbsp	butter	60 mL
½	red bell pepper, diced	½
½	yellow bell pepper, diced	½
1 tbsp	chopped fresh rosemary	15 mL
1 tbsp	chopped fresh chives	15 mL
1 tbsp	chopped fresh parsley	15 mL
	salt and freshly ground pepper	

~ Preheat oven to 300°F (150°C). Heat 1 tbsp (15 mL) olive oil in a large frying pan over medium-high heat. Add tuna steaks and cook 2 minutes on each side. Remove from pan and keep warm in oven.

~ Add 1 tbsp (15 mL) of olive oil to the pan, increase heat to high and sauté portabella mushrooms 3 minutes on each side. Season and set aside with tuna. Add remaining oil and sauté oyster mushrooms 3 minutes on each side, and set aside in oven.

~ Melt butter in frying pan. Add peppers and herbs; mix well. Serve tuna steaks with mushrooms and herb butter.

4 SERVINGS

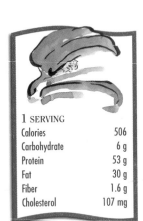

1 SERVING	
Calories	506
Carbohydrate	6 g
Protein	53 g
Fat	30 g
Fiber	1.6 g
Cholesterol	107 mg

EEL À LA PROVENÇALE

2 tbsp	olive oil	30 mL
1⅓ lbs	eel, skinned, cut in 1 inch (2.5 cm) sections	600 g
½ cup	dry white wine	125 mL
6	tomatoes, peeled, seeded and diced	6
3	garlic cloves, chopped	3
2 tbsp	chopped fresh parsley	30 mL
2 tbsp	chopped fresh thyme	30 mL
	salt and freshly ground pepper	

≈ In a large frying pan, heat olive oil over medium heat. Season sections of eel and sauté 3 minutes. Add white wine and cook to thicken sauce.

≈ Reduce heat to low. Add tomatoes, garlic, parsley and thyme; season and continue cooking 10 minutes.

≈ Serve with fried potato slices.

4 SERVINGS

*NOTE: EELS LAY THEIR EGGS IN THE SARGASSO SEA. THE LARVAE, OR LEPTOCEPHALI, ARE CARRIED BY GULF STREAM CURRENTS TO THE EUROPEAN COAST WHERE THEY SWIM UP STREAMS AND RIVERS. THIS VOYAGE TAKES 2 TO 3 YEARS.

1 SERVING	
Calories	458
Carbohydrate	10 g
Protein	37 g
Fat	30 g
Fiber	2.4 g
Cholesterol	242 mg

*NOTE: TURMERIC HAS BEEN USED IN COOKING FOR MORE THAN 2,600 YEARS. LIKE GINGER ROOT, IT COMES FROM A TROPICAL PLANT. IT IS RELATED TO SAFFRON AND IS JUST AS COLORFUL, BUT IT IS MORE BITTER TASTING.

SINGAPORE SHRIMP

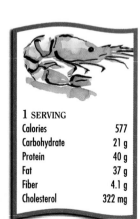

1 SERVING	
Calories	577
Carbohydrate	21 g
Protein	40 g
Fat	37 g
Fiber	4.1 g
Cholesterol	322 mg

2	red chili peppers, seeded	2
6	dry shallots	6
4	garlic cloves	4
1	2-inch (5 cm) piece fresh ginger, peeled	1
1	1-inch (2.5 cm) piece fresh turmeric, peeled	1
1	lemon grass stalk, chopped	1
2 tbsp	tomato purée	30 mL
½ cup	water	125 mL
2 tbsp	peanut oil	30 mL
1½ lbs	large fresh shrimp, peeled and deveined, tails intact	675 g
2 cups	coconut cream	500 mL
	sea salt	

~ Place chili peppers, shallots, garlic, ginger, turmeric, lemon grass, tomato purée and water in blender; blend into a purée.

~ Heat oil in a large frying pan over high heat. Cook shrimp (in two batches, if necessary) 2 minutes; remove and set aside.

~ Add purée to pan and bring to a boil. Add coconut cream and simmer 5 minutes. Correct seasoning and serve shrimp with sauce and egg noodles.

4 SERVINGS

STIR-FRIED CARP WITH SNOW PEAS

1 tbsp	vegetable oil	15 mL
1 lb	carp fillets, skinned and sliced	450 g
2	onions, halved and sliced	2
1	2-inch (5 cm) piece fresh ginger root, cut in julienne	1
2	garlic cloves, chopped	2
½ lb	snow peas	225 g
1	red bell pepper, sliced	1
1	yellow bell pepper, sliced	1
¼ cup	soy sauce	50 mL
2 tbsp	sherry	30 mL
2 tbsp	chopped garlic chives	30 mL

≈ Heat frying pan or wok over high heat. Add oil and stir-fry carp 1 minute.

≈ Add onions, ginger and garlic; continue cooking 2 minutes. Add snow peas and red and yellow peppers; cook 2 minutes.

≈ Pour in soy sauce, sherry and garlic chives. Mix well and serve immediately.

4 SERVINGS

*NOTE: THE TASTE OF CARP, MORE THAN THAT OF ANY OTHER FISH, IS DIRECTLY RELATED TO ITS HABITAT. BECAUSE IT LIVES IN SHALLOW WATERS LIKE LAKES AND PONDS, ITS FLESH MAY HAVE A 'MUDDY' TASTE. THAT IS WHY FARMED CARP IS OFTEN BETTER.

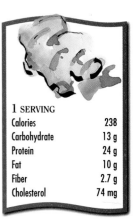

1 SERVING	
Calories	238
Carbohydrate	13 g
Protein	24 g
Fat	10 g
Fiber	2.7 g
Cholesterol	74 mg

SALMON STEAKS WITH ENDIVE AND BASIL SAUCE

2 tbsp	olive oil	30 mL
4	salmon steaks, about 6 oz (175 g) each	4
4	dry shallots, chopped	4
4	Belgian endives, sliced	4
1 cup	dry white wine	250 mL
½ cup	fish stock	125 mL
1 cup	heavy cream (35% MF)	250 mL
1 cup	basil leaves	250 mL
	sea salt and freshly ground pepper	

∼ Preheat oven to 200°F (100°C).

∼ Heat oil in a large frying pan over high heat. Reduce heat to medium and cook salmon steaks 5 minutes on each side. Remove steaks and keep warm in oven.

∼ Add shallots and endives to pan and cook 3 minutes (add a little oil if necessary). Add wine and fish stock; simmer until sauce is reduced by half.

∼ Add cream and cook 5 minutes over medium heat. Season and add basil leaves; continue cooking 2 minutes. Top salmon steaks with sauce and serve with rice, if desired.

4 SERVINGS

*NOTE: TO PREVENT ENDIVES FROM TURNING GREEN, KEEP THEM IN A DARK PLACE, OR IN THE BLUE PAPER THAT THEY ARE OFTEN PACKAGED IN.

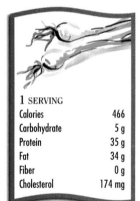

1 SERVING	
Calories	466
Carbohydrate	5 g
Protein	35 g
Fat	34 g
Fiber	0 g
Cholesterol	174 mg

SAUTÉED SHRIMP WITH AÏOLI

1	**red bell pepper, halved and seeded**	1
4	**garlic cloves, finely chopped**	4
1	**egg yolk**	1
1 cup + 2 tbsp	**extra virgin olive oil**	280 mL
1½ lbs	**fresh medium shrimp, peeled and deveined, tails intact**	675 g
	juice of 1 lemon	
	toasted French bread	
	salt and freshly ground pepper	

∼ Preheat oven to 400°F (200°C). Oil bell pepper halves and place cut-side-down on cookie sheet. Cook 15 minutes in oven. Place in a bowl, cover with plastic wrap and let cool 10 minutes.

∼ Remove skin from peppers and purée in blender. Add garlic and egg yolk; purée. Gradually add 1 cup (250 mL) of oil, blending well after each addition. Aïoli should become very thick. Add lemon juice and season.

∼ Heat 1 tbsp (15 mL) oil in a large frying pan over high heat. Cook half of shrimp 2 minutes on each side; remove and set aside. Add remaining oil and cook second batch of shrimp.

∼ Serve shrimp with fresh green beans and toasted French bread with red aïoli.

4 SERVINGS

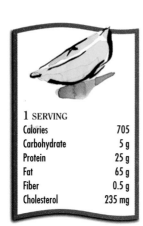

1 SERVING	
Calories	705
Carbohydrate	5 g
Protein	25 g
Fat	65 g
Fiber	0.5 g
Cholesterol	235 mg

*NOTE: TO KEEP SHRIMP FRESH, RINSE WELL IN COLD WATER, DRAIN AND PLACE THEM IN AN AIRTIGHT CONTAINER IN THE REFRIGERATOR. THEY WILL KEEP 2 DAYS.

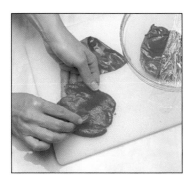

Peel cooled bell peppers.

In a blender, purée bell peppers and add garlic and egg yolk.

Gradually blend in 1 cup (250 mL) olive oil.

RED MULLET WITH MUSHROOM AND THYME SAUCE

1 tbsp	peanut oil	15 mL
2 lbs	unskinned red mullet fillets	900 g
2 tbsp	butter	30 mL
1	leek, white part only, diced	1
2	dry shallots, chopped	2
½ lb	mushrooms, diced	225 g
½	red bell pepper, diced	½
1 cup	chicken stock	250 mL
2 tbsp	chopped fresh thyme	30 mL
	salt and freshly ground pepper	

∼ Heat oil in a large frying pan over high heat and cook fillets about 2 minutes on each side, beginning with skin side. Remove and set aside.

∼ Add 1 tbsp (15 mL) of butter to pan. Add leek and shallots and cook 2 minutes. Add mushrooms and red pepper; continue cooking 2 minutes. Pour in chicken stock, add remaining butter and thyme; correct seasoning.

∼ Return fillets to sauce and serve.

4 SERVINGS

*NOTE: LEEKS ARE EASIER TO CLEAN IF THEY ARE FIRST CUT INTO FOUR, LEAVING ABOUT 1 INCH (2.5 CM) INTACT AT BASE.

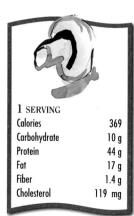

1 SERVING	
Calories	369
Carbohydrate	10 g
Protein	44 g
Fat	17 g
Fiber	1.4 g
Cholesterol	119 mg

DOVER SOLE WITH SHALLOTS AND ORANGE

4	whole Dover soles (about 7 oz/200g each)	4
5 tbsp	clarified butter	75 mL
4	dry shallots, chopped	4
2 tbsp	chopped fresh chervil	30 mL
	zest of 1 orange, in fine julienne	
	juice of 2 oranges	
	salt and freshly ground pepper	

~ Season Dover soles. Melt 1 tbsp (15 mL) of butter in a large frying pan over medium heat. Sauté fish, one at a time, 5 minutes on each side over medium-high heat, adding 1 tbsp (15 mL) of butter for each fish. Remove from pan and keep warm.

~ Melt remaining butter in pan over medium heat. Sauté shallots 1 minute. Add chervil, orange zest and orange juice; mix well. Pour over sole and serve.

4 SERVINGS

*NOTE: THE ZEST IS THE COLORED PEEL OF THE FRUIT. THE WHITE PART OF THE PEEL IS BITTER. DO NOT USE IT WHEN PREPARING THE ZEST.

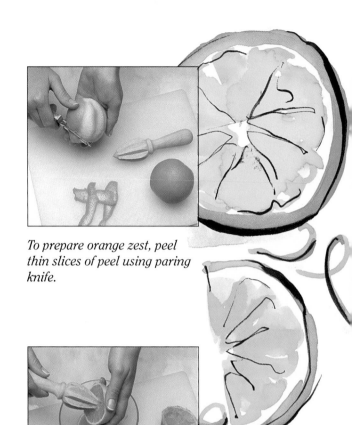

To prepare orange zest, peel thin slices of peel using paring knife.

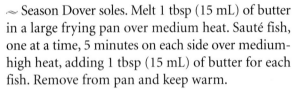

Squeeze oranges for juice.

Using sharp knife, cut slices of orange peel into fine julienne.

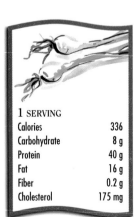

1 SERVING	
Calories	336
Carbohydrate	8 g
Protein	40 g
Fat	16 g
Fiber	0.2 g
Cholesterol	175 mg

SQUID WITH GARLIC AND BLACK PEPPERCORNS

1¾ lbs	fresh squid	800 g
2 tbsp	olive oil	30 mL
3	garlic cloves, chopped	3
1 tbsp	crushed black peppercorns	15 mL
2 tbsp	chopped fresh parsley	30 mL
	juice of 1 lemon	
	sea salt	

∽ Prepare squid as shown on page 12. Slice each squid lengthwise in two and make small crisscross incisions on each piece.

∽ Heat oil in a frying pan over medium heat. Sauté squid (in two batches) 2 minutes, turning over several times.

∽ Return all squid to pan. Add garlic and pepper; cook 1 minute. Add parsley and lemon juice; mix well. Correct seasoning and serve hot.

4 SERVINGS

1 SERVING	
Calories	254
Carbohydrate	9 g
Protein	32 g
Fat	10 g
Fiber	0.2 g
Cholesterol	466 mg

*NOTE: BALSAMIC VINEGAR
COMES FROM ITALY.
PRODUCED FROM THE WHITE
GRAPE, IT IS LEFT TO AGE IN
THE BARREL, WHICH GIVES IT
A DARKER COLOR.

SALMON WITH HAZELNUTS AND WATERCRESS

½ cup	whole hazelnuts	125 mL
4	unskinned salmon fillets, about ⅓ lb (150 g) each	4
2 tbsp	olive oil	30 mL
4 tsp	balsamic vinegar	20 mL
4 tbsp	extra virgin olive oil	60 mL
2	bunches watercress	2
	salt and freshly ground pepper	

∾ Preheat oven to 375°F (190°C). Place hazelnuts on baking sheet and toast in oven about 6 minutes, or until lightly golden. Remove from oven and let cool; chop coarsely and set aside.

∾ Season fish on both sides. Heat oil in large frying pan over high heat. Add salmon, skin-side-down, and cook 5 minutes over medium-high heat. Turn salmon over and cook 5 minutes over medium heat. Turn fish over again and cook 2 to 5 minutes, or until cooked as desired.

∾ Combine balsamic vinegar and extra virgin olive oil. Toss watercress and hazelnuts with vinaigrette and season well. Serve salmon with watercress and hazelnut salad.

4 SERVINGS

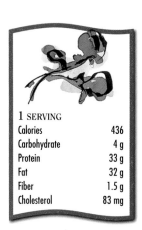

1 SERVING	
Calories	436
Carbohydrate	4 g
Protein	33 g
Fat	32 g
Fiber	1.5 g
Cholesterol	83 mg

SCALLOPS WITH PECORINO PESTO

1½ cups	fresh basil leaves	375 mL
3	garlic cloves, coarsely chopped	3
½ cup	grated Pecorino cheese	125 mL
½ cup	grated Parmesan cheese	125 mL
1 cup + 2 tbsp	olive oil	280 mL
1¼ lbs	fresh scallops	550 g
½ lb	fresh portabella mushrooms, sliced	225 g
	salt and freshly ground pepper	
	juice of ½ lemon	
	fresh cooked pasta of your choice	

≈ Place basil, garlic and both cheeses in blender or food processor; blend to combine. Gradually add 1 cup (250 mL) olive oil, blending well after each addition. Set pesto sauce aside.

≈ Heat 1 tbsp (15 mL) of olive oil in frying pan over high heat. Season scallops and cook 1 minute on each side. Remove scallops and set aside.

≈ Add remaining oil to pan. Season mushrooms with salt and pepper and cook over high heat about 4 minutes.

≈ Return scallops to frying pan, add lemon juice and simmer 2 minutes over low heat. Serve with pesto sauce and fresh cooked pasta.

4 SERVINGS

*NOTE: PECORINO IS AN ITALIAN CHEESE MADE FROM EWES' MILK, WHILE PARMESAN, ALSO ITALIAN, IS FROM COWS' MILK. BOTH ARE HARD, GRANULAR-TYPE CHEESES USED MAINLY FOR GRATING.

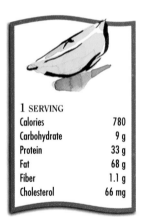

1 SERVING	
Calories	780
Carbohydrate	9 g
Protein	33 g
Fat	68 g
Fiber	1.1 g
Cholesterol	66 mg

*NOTE: TOMATILLOS ARE FROM MEXICO AND CENTRAL AMERICA. GENERALLY IT IS THE GREEN TOMATILLOS, YELLOW WHEN FULLY RIPENED, THAT ARE USED IN COOKING.

BLUEFISH FILLETS WITH TOMATILLO SAUCE ⁓

1 lb	tomatillos*	450 g
2	green onions, chopped	2
1	garlic clove, coarsely chopped	1
2 tbsp	chopped fresh cilantro	30 mL
1	jalapeño pepper, finely chopped	1
½	red bell pepper, finely chopped	½
4	unskinned bluefish fillets, about 7 oz (200 g) each	4
2 tbsp	peanut oil	30 mL
	juice of 2 limes	
	cherry tomatoes for garnish	
	salt and freshly ground pepper	

⁓ Remove hull (membrane) from tomatillos and cook in boiling salted water 10 minutes.

⁓ Drain tomatillos and purée in blender or food processor along with green onions, garlic, cilantro, jalapeño pepper and lime juice. Stir in red bell pepper, season and set aside.

⁓ Cut each fillet in 2 and season. Heat peanut oil in frying pan over high heat and cook fish 3 minutes on each side. Serve bluefish over tomatillo sauce and garnish with cherry tomatoes.

4 SERVINGS

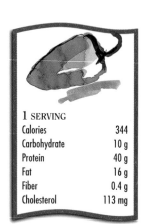

1 SERVING	
Calories	344
Carbohydrate	10 g
Protein	40 g
Fat	16 g
Fiber	0.4 g
Cholesterol	113 mg

Sautéed Swordfish with Diced Vegetables

3 tbsp	olive oil	45 mL
1	onion, diced	1
1	small eggplant, diced	1
1	green zucchini, diced	1
1	yellow zucchini, diced	1
1	red bell pepper, diced	1
2	garlic cloves, finely chopped	2
1 tbsp	chopped fresh thyme	15 mL
4	swordfish steaks, about 6 oz (175 g) each	4
	sea salt and freshly ground pepper	
	basil oil (see recipe page 252)	

~ To prepare the vegetables, heat 2 tbsp (30 mL) olive oil in a large frying pan over medium-high heat. Add onion and eggplant and cook 3 minutes. Add green and yellow zucchini and cook 2 more minutes. Add red pepper and garlic; cook 2 minutes. Season and add fresh thyme; mix and set aside.

~ Season fish on both sides. Heat remaining oil over medium-high heat and cook fish 4 to 5 minutes on each side.

~ Sprinkle basil oil on swordfish, and serve with vegetables and crusty French bread.

4 SERVINGS

*NOTE: THE GREEN SPROUT AT THE CENTER OF A CLOVE OF GARLIC IS BITTER AND DIFFICULT TO DIGEST. IT SHOULD THEREFORE BE REMOVED.

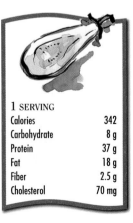

1 SERVING	
Calories	342
Carbohydrate	8 g
Protein	37 g
Fat	18 g
Fiber	2.5 g
Cholesterol	70 mg

TURBOT À LA MEUNIÈRE WITH TOASTED ALMONDS ~

½ cup	slivered almonds	125 mL
½ cup	all-purpose flour	125 mL
1 lb	turbot fillets	450 g
4 tbsp	clarified butter	60 mL
2 tbsp	chopped fresh parsley	30 mL
	juice of 1 lemon	
	salt and freshly ground pepper	

~ Preheat oven to 375°F (190°C). Place almonds on a baking sheet and toast in oven 3 to 4 minutes, or until golden. Season flour; dredge turbot fillets in flour.

~ Heat 1 tbsp (15 mL) clarified butter in large frying pan over high heat. Reduce heat to medium-high and cook fillets 2 minutes on each side. Transfer fish to serving platter.

~ Place remaining butter, parsley, lemon juice and roasted almonds in frying pan. Mix well until heated through and pour over fish. Serve immediately, garnished with lemon slices.

4 SERVINGS

*NOTE: BUTTER WILL ABSORB ODORS. IT IS BEST TO KEEP IT IN AN AIRTIGHT CONTAINER IN THE REFRIGERATOR. SALTED BUTTER WILL KEEP 1 MONTH; UNSALTED BUTTER WILL KEEP 2 WEEKS.

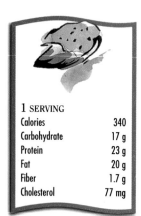

1 SERVING	
Calories	340
Carbohydrate	17 g
Protein	23 g
Fat	20 g
Fiber	1.7 g
Cholesterol	77 mg

~~~~~~~~~~~~~~~~~~~~~~

*NOTE: READY TO USE CAJUN SPICE MIX CAN BE FOUND IN MOST GROCERY STORES AND SUPERMARKETS. IT IS USUALLY MADE WITH GARLIC, ONION, CHILI PEPPERS, BLACK PEPPER, MUSTARD AND CELERY.

BLACKENED CAJUN POMPANO ~

1 tbsp	paprika	15 mL
1 tsp	Cayenne pepper	5 mL
1 tbsp	Cajun spice mix*	15 mL
4	pompano fillets, about 6 oz (175 g) each	4
2 tbsp	peanut oil	30 mL
	sea salt	

~ Mix together paprika, Cayenne pepper and Cajun spice. Season fillets on both sides with salt and dredge in spices.

~ Heat oil in a large frying pan over high heat and cook fillets about 4 minutes on each side. Fish should be black when done. Serve pompano fillets with new potatoes and fresh corn, if desired.

4 SERVINGS

1 SERVING	
Calories	369
Carbohydrate	2 g
Protein	34 g
Fat	25 g
Fiber	0 g
Cholesterol	90 mg

CHINESE FISH AND SEAFOOD STIR-FRY

2 tbsp	vegetable oil	30 mL
1	green bell pepper, cubed	1
3	celery stalks, sliced	3
1	head of broccoli, in florets	1
⅔ lb	monkfish (anglerfish) fillets, cut in sections	300 g
½ lb	fresh shrimp	225 g
⅔ lb	crab legs, chopped	300 g
2	garlic cloves, finely chopped	2
4	green onions, chopped	4
1 tsp	cornstarch	5 mL
2 tbsp	soy sauce	30 mL
⅓ cup	water	75 mL
1 tbsp	brown sugar	15 mL
1 tsp	chili paste	5 mL
1 tsp	sesame oil	5 mL

~ Heat wok over medium-high heat; when hot, add oil. Increase heat to high and sauté green pepper, celery and broccoli 2 minutes. Remove vegetables and set aside.

~ Over high heat, cook monkfish in wok 2 minutes. Add shrimp and crab legs; cook 2 more minutes. Return vegetables to wok and add garlic and green onions. Mix well and cook 2 minutes.

~ In a bowl, combine cornstarch, soy sauce, water, brown sugar, chili paste and sesame oil. Add mixture to the wok and cook 2 minutes, or until sauce thickens. Sprinkle with sesame seeds, if desired, and serve.

4 SERVINGS

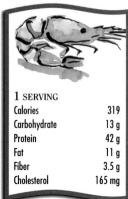

1 SERVING	
Calories	319
Carbohydrate	13 g
Protein	42 g
Fat	11 g
Fiber	3.5 g
Cholesterol	165 mg

Sauté vegetables in a wok over high heat.

Cook monkfish over high heat.

Add shrimp and crab legs.

~~~~~~~~~~~

*NOTE: MONKFISH (ALSO KNOWN AS ANGLERFISH) HAS LEAN, TASTY FLESH. IT IS OFTEN PREPARED JUST LIKE MEAT AND CAN BE SAUTÉED, GRILLED OR BAKED.

Return vegetables to wok.

Add garlic and green onions.

Add soy sauce mixture to wok and cook 2 minutes, or until sauce thickens.

ITALIAN-STYLE SCAMPI

2 tbsp	olive oil	30 mL
32	small scampi,* peeled and deveined	32
3	dry shallots, chopped	3
2	garlic cloves, chopped	2
½ cup	dry white wine	125 mL
6	large tomatoes, peeled, seeded and chopped	6
2 tbsp	chopped fresh basil	30 mL
	salt and freshly ground pepper	

~ Heat oil in frying pan over high heat. Add scampi and season well. Cook 2 minutes, stirring once. Remove scampi from pan and set aside.

~ Add shallots and garlic to hot pan; cook 1 minute. Pour in wine and continue cooking 2 minutes. Stir in tomatoes and basil; season well and cook 6 to 8 minutes over medium-low heat.

~ Return scampi to pan and mix well. Correct seasoning, simmer 2 minutes and serve.

4 SERVINGS

*NOTE: SCAMPI IS A TYPE OF LARGE SHRIMP. SCAMPI FRITTI (FRIED IN BATTER) IS A POPULAR ITALIAN PREPARATION.

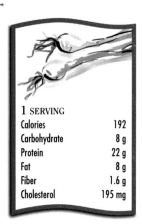

1 SERVING	
Calories	192
Carbohydrate	8 g
Protein	22 g
Fat	8 g
Fiber	1.6 g
Cholesterol	195 mg

$\mathcal{B}$RAISED

It is hard to resist the exquisite taste of fish or

seafood that has simmered over a bed of vegetables.

Infused with the subtle aroma of fresh herbs, the

taste is ever more delicious.

This chapter offers a selection of recipes to suit

every occasion and appetite. They are all quick

and easy to prepare, and the results speak for

themselves.

SAFFRON SEAFOOD STEW

1 cup	dry white wine	250 mL
4 tbsp	olive oil	60 mL
2	leeks, white part only, halved and sliced	2
2	garlic cloves, chopped	2
2	pinches saffron	2
1 tbsp	tomato paste	15 mL
6 cups	fish stock	1.5 L
2	crabs, cut in four	2
12	large shrimp, peeled and deveined	12
½ lb	sea bass fillets	225 g
6	Italian tomatoes, peeled, seeded and chopped	6
1	red bell pepper, diced	1
8	mussels, washed, scrubbed and bearded	8
8	clams, washed	8
1 tbsp	chopped fresh basil	15 mL
1 tbsp	chopped fresh thyme	15 mL
1 tbsp	chopped fresh rosemary	15 mL
	salt and freshly ground pepper	

∼ Pour wine into a large stewpot. Add olive oil, leeks and garlic; cover and cook 6 to 7 minutes over medium heat. Add saffron, tomato paste and fish stock; bring to a boil.

∼ Add crabs and cook 8 minutes over medium heat. Add shrimp, sea bass, tomatoes and red pepper; continue cooking 5 minutes.

∼ Place mussels and clams on top, cover and cook 5 minutes or until shells open. Discard any mussels or clams that do not open.

∼ Add fresh herbs, correct seasoning and serve.

4 SERVINGS

*NOTE: SEA BASS IS KNOWN AS 'LOUP DE MER' (SEA WOLF) BECAUSE IT IS A FEROCIOUS PREDATOR. IT HAS VERY LEAN, FINE FLESH.

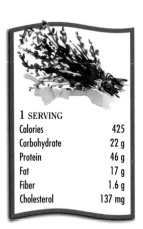

1 SERVING	
Calories	425
Carbohydrate	22 g
Protein	46 g
Fat	17 g
Fiber	1.6 g
Cholesterol	137 mg

BENGALI CURRY WITH HADDOCK

2 tbsp	ghee (clarified butter)	30 mL
1	onion, finely chopped	1
1 tsp	ground cumin	5 mL
1 tsp	ground coriander	5 mL
1 tsp	ground turmeric	5 mL
1 tbsp	garam masala*	15 mL
2	garlic cloves, finely chopped	2
2 tsp	tomato paste	10 mL
1½ cups	coconut cream	375 mL
1¼ lbs	haddock fillets, cubed	550 g
	salt and freshly ground pepper	

≈ In a medium saucepan, melt ghee over medium heat. Add onion, cumin, coriander and turmeric; cook 3 minutes, stirring constantly. Add garam masala, garlic and tomato paste. Mix well.

≈ Add coconut cream, correct seasoning and let simmer 8 minutes. Add haddock fillets, cover and cook 7 minutes. Serve with naan bread, green beans and basmati rice, if desired.

4 SERVINGS

*****NOTE:** GARAM MASALA IS A MIX OF SPICES USED EXTENSIVELY IN THE CUISINE OF NORTHERN INDIA. IT IS GENERALLY MADE WITH BLACK AND WHITE CUMIN SEEDS, CORIANDER SEEDS, BLACK CARDAMOM, BAY LEAVES, BLACK PEPPERCORNS, GRATED NUTMEG, WHOLE CLOVES AND CINNAMON STICKS. THESE INGREDIENTS ARE FRIED AND THEN GROUND INTO A FINE POWDER.

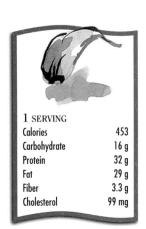

1 SERVING	
Calories	453
Carbohydrate	16 g
Protein	32 g
Fat	29 g
Fiber	3.3 g
Cholesterol	99 mg

MONKFISH PAPRIKACHE

1 tbsp	olive oil	15 mL
2	onions, finely chopped	2
1 tbsp	paprika	15 mL
1⅓ lbs	monkfish (anglerfish), cut in large cubes	600 g
3	garlic cloves, chopped	3
1 cup	fish stock	250 mL
8	tomatoes, peeled, seeded and chopped	8
2 tbsp	tomato paste	30 mL
6 tbsp	sour cream	90 mL
2 tbsp	chopped fresh parsley	30 mL
	salt and freshly ground pepper	

∼ Heat oil in a large frying pan over medium heat. Add onions and paprika and cook 10 minutes. Season monkfish and add to frying pan along with garlic; toss well.

∼ Pour in fish stock and bring to a boil. Reduce heat to low and stir in tomatoes and tomato paste. Season well, cover and cook 20 minutes.

∼ Add sour cream and chopped parsley; mix and serve hot.

4 SERVINGS

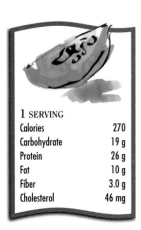

1 SERVING	
Calories	270
Carbohydrate	19 g
Protein	26 g
Fat	10 g
Fiber	3.0 g
Cholesterol	46 mg

Sauté onions and paprika 10 minutes.

Add seasoned monkfish and garlic.

Pour in fish stock.

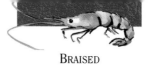

~~~~~~~~~~~~

*NOTE: PAPRIKACHE IS A HUNGARIAN STEW MADE WITH WHITE MEAT OR FISH, PAPRIKA AND SOUR CREAM. PAPRIKA VARIES IN TASTE FROM HOT TO MILD AND SWEET, AND IN APPEARANCE FROM ROSY BROWN TO SCARLET.

Add chopped tomatoes.

Stir in tomato paste.

Add sour cream and chopped parsley just before serving.

SHRIMP WITH CARAMELIZED ONIONS

2 tbsp	olive oil	30 mL
4	onions, halved and sliced	4
2	garlic cloves, chopped	2
¼ cup	dry white wine	50 mL
½ cup	chicken stock	125 mL
1 tbsp	chopped fresh thyme	15 mL
1⅓ lbs	fresh medium shrimp, peeled and deveined	600 g
	salt and freshly ground pepper	

≈ Heat oil in a medium saucepan over medium-low heat. Add onions and cook 10 minutes, or until onions are golden. Add garlic and white wine; continue cooking 3 minutes. Add chicken stock, season and cook 5 minutes.

≈ Add thyme and shrimp and cook 5 minutes over medium heat. Serve with steamed rice and sautéed rapini, if desired.

4 SERVINGS

*NOTE: ONIONS ARE LOW IN CALORIES AND RICH IN SULPHUR AND VITAMIN C. RAW, THEY MAY BE DIFFICULT TO DIGEST.

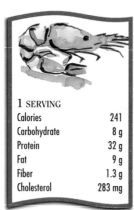

1 SERVING	
Calories	241
Carbohydrate	8 g
Protein	32 g
Fat	9 g
Fiber	1.3 g
Cholesterol	283 mg

*NOTE: NUTMEG IS MUCH
MORE FLAVORFUL WHEN IT IS
FRESHLY GRATED.

SKATE WITH LEMON AND NUTMEG

3 tbsp	butter	45 mL
2	dry shallots, chopped	2
½ cup	dry white wine	125 mL
1 cup	fish stock	250 mL
1 tbsp	freshly grated nutmeg	15 mL
4	skate wings, about ¼ lb (115 g) each	4
1	lemon, peeled and chopped	1
1 tbsp	chopped fresh thyme	15 mL
	juice of 1 lemon	
	sea salt and freshly ground pepper	

≈ Melt 1 tbsp (15 mL) of butter in a frying pan and sauté shallots 2 minutes over medium heat. Add wine, bring to a boil and cook 2 minutes. Add fish stock and nutmeg.

≈ Season skate and place in frying pan, 2 wings at a time. Cover and cook 7 minutes over medium heat.

≈ Remove fish and keep warm. To the cooking liquid, add remaining butter, lemon juice, chopped lemon and thyme; cook 1 minute. Serve skate with lemon and nutmeg sauce.

4 SERVINGS

1 SERVING	
Calories	222
Carbohydrate	5 g
Protein	28 g
Fat	10 g
Fiber	0.3 g
Cholesterol	37 mg

185

*NOTE: To hard-boil eggs without breaking the shell, place them in a saucepan of cold water, bring to a boil and cook about 10 minutes. Plunge boiled eggs 7 to 8 minutes in cold water. Remove the shell while they are still warm.

Sauté onion.

Add chopped squid heads and garlic.

Combine breadcrumbs, Parmesan cheese, eggs, anchovies, pine nuts, remaining olive oil and onion mixture.

STUFFED SQUID IN CORIANDER SAUCE

8	fresh squid, about 3½ oz (100 g) each	8
3 tbsp	olive oil	45 mL
1	onion, finely chopped	1
2	garlic cloves, chopped	2
½ cup	breadcrumbs	125 mL
½ cup	grated Parmesan cheese	125 mL
2	hard-boiled eggs, chopped	2
2	anchovies, chopped	2
3 tbsp	pine nuts, toasted and chopped	45 mL
3 cups	tomato purée	750 mL
2 tbsp	chopped fresh coriander	30 mL
	salt and freshly ground pepper	

≈ Prepare squid as shown on page 12. Chop squid heads. Heat 1 tbsp (15 mL) olive oil in a frying pan over medium heat. Sauté onion 5 minutes. Add squid heads and garlic; cook 1 minute.

≈ In a bowl, combine breadcrumbs, Parmesan cheese, eggs, anchovies, pine nuts and remaining olive oil. Add onion and squid mixture, season with pepper and mix well. Stuff squid bodies with mixture and keep closed with toothpicks.

≈ Heat tomato purée over medium heat; carefully place stuffed squid in purée. Let simmer 3 minutes, turn squid over and cook 2 minutes. Add fresh coriander, correct seasoning and serve immediately.

4 SERVINGS

1 SERVING	
Calories	536
Carbohydrate	35 g
Protein	45 g
Fat	24 g
Fiber	3.2 g
Cholesterol	584 mg

Stuff squid with mixture.

Keep closed with toothpicks.

Place stuffed squid in tomato purée.

MADRAS CURRY SCALLOPS

2 tbsp	ghee (clarified butter)	30 mL
3	dry shallots, finely chopped	3
2 tbsp	Madras curry powder*	30 mL
1 tsp	ground turmeric	5 mL
1 tsp	all-purpose flour	5 mL
1 cup	fish stock	250 mL
½ cup	coconut cream	125 mL
1¼ lbs	fresh scallops	550 g

≈ Heat ghee in frying pan over medium heat. Add shallots and cook 3 minutes over low heat. Sprinkle in curry powder and turmeric; mix well. Continue cooking 2 minutes, stirring frequently.

≈ Add flour and cook 1 minute. Stir in fish stock and cook 2 minutes over medium heat. Add coconut cream and cook 10 minutes. Add scallops, mix well and simmer 4 minutes. Serve with green beans and red potatoes.

4 SERVINGS

*NOTE: EVERY REGION OF INDIA HAS ITS OWN MIXTURE OF SPICES THAT IS USED TO MAKE CURRY. MADRAS CURRY POWDER IS GENERALLY MADE WITH HOT PEPPERS, CORIANDER SEEDS, CUMIN SEEDS, GINGER, BLACK MUSTARD SEEDS, FENUGREEK, TURMERIC AND BLACK PEPPER.

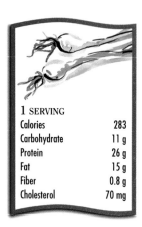

1 SERVING	
Calories	283
Carbohydrate	11 g
Protein	26 g
Fat	15 g
Fiber	0.8 g
Cholesterol	70 mg

~~~~~~~~~~~~~~~~~~~~~~

*NOTE: THE LARGEST SWORDFISH ON RECORD WAS CAUGHT WITH A FISHING POLE OFF THE COAST OF CHILE. IT WEIGHED MORE THAN 1100 LBS (500 KG)!

BRAISED SWORDFISH WITH TOMATO SAUCE ~

2 tbsp	olive oil	30 mL
10	Italian tomatoes, peeled and sliced	10
2	garlic cloves, peeled and sliced	2
½ cup	tomato purée	125 mL
2 tbsp	chopped fresh oregano	30 mL
4	swordfish steaks, about 6 oz (175 g) each	4
	salt and freshly ground pepper	

~ Heat oil in heavy frying pan over medium heat. Add tomatoes and cook 8 minutes over low heat.

~ Add garlic, tomato purée and oregano; season well and cook 5 minutes over medium heat.

~ Season fish on both sides, add to pan and cover. Cook 5 minutes on each side, or adjust time depending on thickness. Serve with tomato sauce and sliced zucchini, if desired.

4 SERVINGS

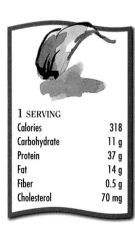

1 SERVING	
Calories	318
Carbohydrate	11 g
Protein	37 g
Fat	14 g
Fiber	0.5 g
Cholesterol	70 mg

GROUPER VERACRUZ ≈

1 tbsp	olive oil	15 mL
2	onions, thinly sliced	2
1	garlic clove, chopped	1
4	tomatoes, peeled, seeded and chopped	4
¼ tsp	ground cinnamon	1 mL
¼ tsp	ground clove	1 mL
2	jalapeño peppers, seeded and chopped	2
2 tbsp	capers	30 mL
1 lb	grouper fillets, cubed	450 g
12	green olives, quartered	12
12	black olives, quartered	12
	juice and zest of ½ lemon	
	sea salt and freshly ground pepper	

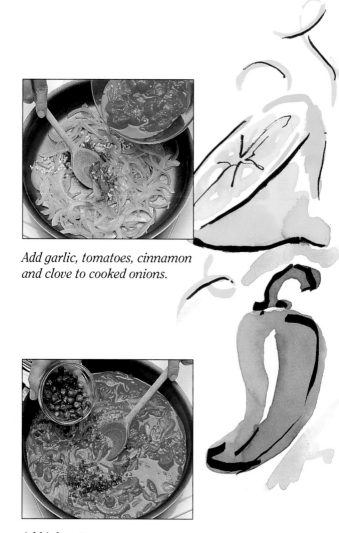

Add garlic, tomatoes, cinnamon and clove to cooked onions.

≈ Heat oil in a frying pan over medium heat. Reduce heat to low, add onions, cover and cook 8 minutes. Add garlic, tomatoes, cinnamon and clove; continue cooking 10 minutes.

≈ Add jalapeño peppers, capers, lemon juice and zest; mix well. Season grouper cubes and add them to frying pan. Cover and cook about 6 minutes. Add olives, correct seasoning and continue cooking 2 minutes. Serve very hot, with rice or potatoes.

4 SERVINGS

Add jalapeño peppers, capers, lemon juice and zest.

*NOTE: TO KEEP OLIVES FRESH, PLACE THEM IN A NON-METALLIC CONTAINER, COVER THEM WITH OIL OR WATER, AND REFRIGERATE.

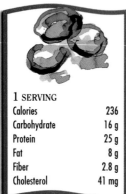

1 SERVING	
Calories	236
Carbohydrate	16 g
Protein	25 g
Fat	8 g
Fiber	2.8 g
Cholesterol	41 mg

Season grouper cubes and add them to frying pan.

BRAISED HALIBUT WITH SESAME AND GINGER

2	onions, sliced	
1	1-inch (2.5 cm) piece fresh ginger, peeled and cut in julienne	
2 tbsp	brown sugar	30 mL
2 tbsp	sesame seeds	30 mL
1 tbsp	sesame oil	15 mL
4 tbsp	soy sauce	60 mL
1 cup	fish stock	250 mL
		100 g
1	carrots, sliced	
	celery, sliced	
1½ lbs	halibut filets	600 g
2 tbsp	chopped fresh chives	30 mL
	salt and freshly ground pepper	

1. Mix together onions, ginger, brown sugar, sesame seeds, sesame oil, soy sauce and fish stock. Pour into a saucepan and cook over medium heat. Add carrots and celery; season with salt and pepper.

2. Season halibut filets. Place them in a large pan. Cook until tender. Sprinkle with fresh chives and serve.

4 servings

~~~~~~~~~~~~~~~~~~~~~~~~~~~~~~~~~~~~

*NOTE: SESAME OIL IS OFTEN USED IN ASIAN CUISINE. THERE ARE SEVERAL VARIETIES. THE LIGHT SESAME OIL HAS A DELICATE, NUTTY FLAVOR. THE DARKER VARIETY, MADE FROM TOASTED SESAME SEEDS, HAS A STRONGER TASTE.

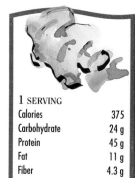

1 SERVING	
Calories	375
Carbohydrate	24 g
Protein	45 g
Fat	11 g
Fiber	4.3 g
Cholesterol	62 mg

*NOTE: BE CAREFUL WHEN CUTTING JALAPEÑO OR OTHER HOT PEPPERS NOT TO TOUCH YOUR EYES OR SKIN; THE PEPPERS CAN BURN THEM. MAKE SURE YOU WEAR GLOVES OR THAT YOU WASH YOUR HANDS THOROUGHLY AFTERWARDS.

LOUISIANA SHARK

4 tbsp	peanut oil	60 mL
2	bay leaves	2
½ cup	finely chopped celery	125 mL
4	shark steaks, about 6 oz (175 g) each	4
2	onions, chopped	2
1 tsp	ground cumin	5 mL
1 tsp	chili powder	5 mL
6	tomatoes, peeled, seeded and chopped	6
1	jalapeño pepper, seeded and finely chopped	1
2	garlic cloves, chopped	2
4	green onions, sliced	4
	juice of 2 limes	
	salt and freshly ground pepper	

≈ In a shallow dish, mix together lime juice, 3 tbsp (45 mL) peanut oil, bay leaves and celery. Add shark steaks and marinate 2 hours.

≈ Heat remaining peanut oil in frying pan over medium heat. Add onions and sauté 3 minutes. Add cumin and chili powder; cook 2 minutes. Add tomatoes, jalapeño pepper and garlic; continue cooking 5 minutes.

≈ Season shark steaks. Place over vegetables in frying pan, cover and cook 20 minutes over low heat. Turn steaks over and continue cooking 15 minutes. Add green onions and correct seasoning; mix well and serve.

4 SERVINGS

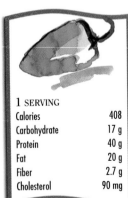

1 SERVING	
Calories	408
Carbohydrate	17 g
Protein	40 g
Fat	20 g
Fiber	2.7 g
Cholesterol	90 mg

MONKFISH AND POTATO FRICASSÉE

2 tbsp	olive oil	30 mL
5	onions, halved and sliced	5
2 cups	fish stock	500 mL
	large potatoes, peeled and sliced	
2	garlic cloves, chopped	2
1½ lbs	monkfish (anglerfish), cut into large chunks	600 g
½ cup	chopped fresh parsley	125 mL
	sea salt and freshly ground pepper	

∼ Heat oil in a large frying pan. Add onions, cover and cook 10 minutes over low heat. Add fish stock, potatoes and garlic. Season and continue cooking 10 minutes.

∼ Season monkfish pieces and place them in the pan; continue cooking 5 minutes. Add parsley, mix well and serve very hot.

4 SERVINGS

∼∼∼∼∼∼∼∼∼∼∼∼∼∼∼

*NOTE: IT IS THE SULFURIC ACID IN ONIONS THAT CAN MAKE YOUR EYES TEAR. TO LESSEN THE EFFECT, PUT THEM IN THE REFRIGERATOR FOR 1 HOUR, OR 10 MINUTES IN THE FREEZER, BEFORE SLICING.

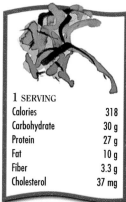

1 SERVING	
Calories	318
Carbohydrate	30 g
Protein	27 g
Fat	10 g
Fiber	3.3 g
Cholesterol	37 mg

IN THE OVEN

Can you think of anything more magnificent than a

baked fish or seafood dish to transform a simple meal

into a gastronomic experience? Prepared in the oven,

fish acquires a unique flavor, texture and appearance

that is sure to tantalize everyone's palate.

Whether baked whole, au gratin, in pies, quiches,

turnovers or rolls, there is no end to the delights

you can create.

FISH AND SEAFOOD PIE

4 cups	fish stock	1 L
2	potatoes, cubed	2
4	carrots, halved and sliced	4
2	leeks, white part only, sliced	2
½ lb	fresh scallops	225 g
½ lb	fresh cod	225 g
3 tbsp	butter	45 mL
3 tbsp	all-purpose flour	45 mL
3	garlic cloves, finely chopped	3
2 tbsp	chopped fresh parsley	30 mL
½ lb	fresh crabmeat	225 g
1 cup	peas	250 mL
½ lb	shortcrust pastry*	225 g
1	egg yolk, beaten	1
	salt and freshly ground pepper	

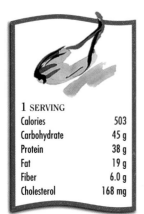

1 SERVING	
Calories	503
Carbohydrate	45 g
Protein	38 g
Fat	19 g
Fiber	6.0 g
Cholesterol	168 mg

~ Pour fish stock into a large saucepan and bring to a boil; add potatoes and cook 5 minutes. Add carrots and leek; continue cooking 5 minutes. Remove vegetables and set aside.

~ Poach scallops and cod in simmering fish stock 2 minutes. Remove and set aside.

~ Preheat oven to 400°F (200°C).

~ Melt butter in another saucepan, add flour and cook 1 minute over low heat. With a whisk, blend in fish stock and bring to a boil, stirring constantly until thick. Add garlic and parsley; season well.

~ Return vegetables, cod, and scallops to sauce; add crabmeat and peas. Mix well and transfer to an ovenproof dish.

~ Roll out pastry to cover the dish. Cut 2 openings in pastry to allow steam to escape, and brush the surface with egg yolk. Bake in oven about 35 minutes, or until pastry is golden.

4 SERVINGS

*NOTE: SHORTCRUST PASTRY IS LIGHT AND FLAKY. IT IS THE CLASSIC BASE FOR TARTS, PATÉS AND PIES. IT CAN BE MADE WITH OR WITHOUT EGGS, AND IS ALSO AVAILABLE FROZEN.

Monkfish Medallions with Kale en Papillote

2 cups	kale, sliced	500 mL
1 lb	monkfish (anglerfish), cleaned and cubed	450 g
4	dry shallots, finely chopped	4
4 tbsp	dry sherry	60 mL
2 tbsp	butter	30 mL
4	fresh thyme sprigs	4
4	pieces parchment paper	4
	sea salt and freshly ground pepper	

∼ Preheat oven to 425°F (220°C).

∼ Blanch kale in salted boiling water about 30 seconds. Plunge in cold water, drain well and pat dry.

∼ Fold each piece of parchment paper in two and cut out a semi-circle. Unfold so you have a circle. Place monkfish cubes on one half of each circle. Cover with kale and shallots, sprinkle with a bit of sherry; add a pat of butter and a thyme sprig. Season well.

∼ Fold the other half of each circle over the filling and roll in the edges to close the packages. Place packages on baking sheet and cook 10 minutes in oven. Serve immediately.

4 SERVINGS

*NOTE: TABLE SALT GENERALLY COMES FROM ROCK SALT IN UNDERGROUND DEPOSITS. SEA SALT, SUPERIOR IN TASTE, CONTAINS MORE MINERALS. IT IS SOLD IN CRYSTALS.

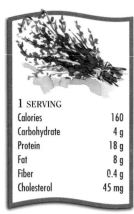

1 SERVING	
Calories	160
Carbohydrate	4 g
Protein	18 g
Fat	8 g
Fiber	0.4 g
Cholesterol	45 mg

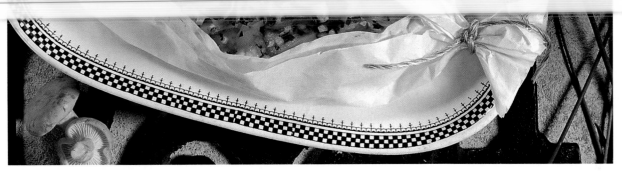

... PAPILLOTE IS USED TO ... COOKED AND SERVED IN PARCHMENT PAPER. SERVE THE PACKAGES AS SOON AS THEY COME OUT OF THE OVEN. DINNER GUESTS WILL ENJOY OPENING THEIR OWN AND BREATHING IN THE RICH AROMA.

STRIPED BASS AND CHANTERELLES EN PAPILLOTE

3 tbsp	butter	45 mL
3½ oz	fresh chanterelle mushrooms, sliced	100 g
4	dry shallots, finely chopped	4
4	striped bass fillets, about ⅓ lb (150 g) each, skinned	4
2 tbsp	chopped fresh chives	30 mL
	juice of ½ lemon	
	sea salt and freshly ground pepper	

≈ Preheat oven to 450°F (230°C).

≈ Melt 1 tbsp (15 mL) butter in frying pan over medium-high heat. Add chanterelles, season and sauté 3 minutes. Add shallots and continue cooking 2 minutes over medium-low heat.

≈ Grease 4 sheets of parchment paper with butter and cover each with some of mushroom mixture. Place fillets on top, 1 for each package, and cover with remaining mushrooms. Sprinkle with lemon juice and chives; season well and top with a pat of butter. Close packages, folding edges to keep juices inside.

≈ Place packages on oiled baking sheet and cook 10 minutes in oven. Remove from oven, transfer to dinner plates and serve.

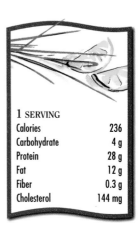

1 SERVING	
Calories	236
Carbohydrate	4 g
Protein	28 g
Fat	12 g
Fiber	0.3 g
Cholesterol	144 mg

4 SERVINGS

TROUT COOKED IN SWISS CHARD LEAVES

4	trout fillets, about 3½ oz (100 g) each, skinned	4
2	dry shallots, chopped	2
2 tbsp	butter	30 mL
6	Swiss chard leaves,* blanched	6
½ cup	dry white wine	125 mL
1 cup	fish stock	250 mL
⅔ cup	heavy cream (35% MF)	150 mL
1 tbsp	butter	15 mL
2	carrots, cut in julienne	2
	sea salt and freshly ground pepper	

～ Season 1 trout fillet. Sprinkle with half of chopped shallots and top with pats of butter. Cover with a second fillet, and cut into 6 pieces. Repeat with remaining fillets.

～ Place each piece of fillet on a Swiss chard leaf and wrap it well. Set packages aside.

～ Preheat oven to 400°F (200°C).

～ Pour white wine and fish stock into an oven-proof dish. Place packages in dish. Cover and cook 12 minutes in oven. Remove packages.

～ Transfer cooking liquid to a small saucepan and cook 5 minutes over medium heat. Add cream, beat with a whisk and continue cooking 5 minutes. Add 1 tbsp (15 mL) butter and beat lightly with a whisk. Serve trout packages with sauce and carrot julienne.

4 SERVINGS

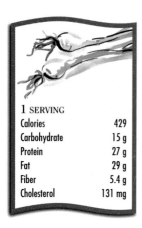

1 SERVING	
Calories	429
Carbohydrate	15 g
Protein	27 g
Fat	29 g
Fiber	5.4 g
Cholesterol	131 mg

Cover garnished trout fillet with another fillet.

Cut into 6 pieces.

Wrap each piece in a Swiss chard leaf.

~~~~~~~~~~~~~

***NOTE:** SWISS CHARD IS A VARIETY OF BEET. THE COOKED LEAVES HAVE A DELICATE FLAVOR. YOU CAN KEEP THEM FRESH IN A PLASTIC BAG IN THE REFRIGERATOR.

Place wrapped pieces of trout in wine and fish stock.

Add cream to cooking liquid and beat with a whisk.

Add butter and whisk lightly.

CLAM QUICHE WITH PANCETTA

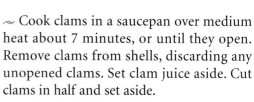

24	fresh clams, washed	24
1 tbsp	butter	15 mL
3½ oz	pancetta,* diced	100 g
1	onion, chopped	1
1	shortcrust pastry pie shell	1
1 cup	grated Provolone cheese	250 mL
¼ cup	heavy cream (35% MF)	50 mL
4	eggs, beaten	4
2 tbsp	chopped fresh chives	30 mL
	salt and freshly ground pepper	

∼ Cook clams in a saucepan over medium heat about 7 minutes, or until they open. Remove clams from shells, discarding any unopened clams. Set clam juice aside. Cut clams in half and set aside.

∼ Melt butter in a frying pan; sauté pancetta 3 minutes over medium heat. Add onion and continue cooking 3 minutes; remove from heat and set aside.

∼ Preheat oven to 375°F (190°C).

∼ Butter and flour a quiche pan and line with pastry. Place pancetta/onion mixture and clams over pastry and sprinkle with cheese. Add enough cream to reserved clam juice to make 1 cup (250 mL); add this liquid to beaten eggs. Season and add chives. Mix well and pour over cheese. Bake quiche in oven about 40 minutes, or until golden.

4 SERVINGS

*NOTE: PANCETTA IS AN ITALIAN BACON THAT IS DRIED WITH SALT AND SPICES BUT NOT SMOKED. IT WILL KEEP 3 WEEKS WRAPPED IN PLASTIC WRAP IN THE REFRIGERATOR, OR 6 MONTHS IN THE FREEZER.

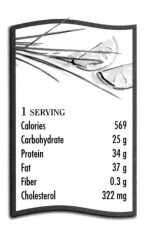

1 SERVING	
Calories	569
Carbohydrate	25 g
Protein	34 g
Fat	37 g
Fiber	0.3 g
Cholesterol	322 mg

*Note: Red mullet is a lean fish, whose flesh is rich in protein, iodine, iron and phosphorous.

Red Mullet in Grapefruit Salsa

2 tbsp	olive oil	30 mL
1	onion, sliced	1
1 tsp	ground coriander	5 mL
1	red bell pepper, diced	1
1	yellow bell pepper, diced	1
1	grapefruit, peeled and sectioned	1
4 tbsp	grapefruit juice	60 mL
2 tbsp	lime juice	30 mL
8	small red mullets, about 3½ oz (100 g) each	8
½ cup	green olives	125 mL
	salt and freshly ground pepper	

~ Preheat oven to 350°F (180°C).

~ Heat oil in a frying pan over medium heat. Add onion and coriander; sauté 3 minutes. Add peppers and continue cooking 2 minutes.

~ Season and add grapefruit sections, grapefruit juice and lime juice.

~ Season red mullet and place in an oven-proof dish. Pour juice over fish and add vegetables. Add olives, cover with aluminum foil and cook 15 minutes in oven.

4 SERVINGS

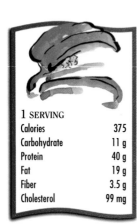

1 SERVING	
Calories	375
Carbohydrate	11 g
Protein	40 g
Fat	19 g
Fiber	3.5 g
Cholesterol	99 mg

POMPANO WITH VEGETABLES AND ROASTED GARLIC

2 tbsp	olive oil	30 mL
8	garlic cloves	8
1	eggplant, diced	1
¼ lb	fresh mushrooms, sliced	225 g
3	tomatoes, seeded and diced	3
1 tbsp	chopped fresh oregano	15 mL
4	pompano fillets, about 6 oz (175 g) each	4

∼ Preheat oven to 450°F (230°C).

∼ Heat olive oil in a saucepan over medium heat. Add garlic cloves and eggplant, season well and cook 4 minutes. Add mushrooms and continue cooking 4 minutes.

∼ Add tomatoes and oregano, correct seasoning. Place vegetables in a rectangular baking dish. Season fillets and place on top of vegetables, in a single layer. Cover with foil and bake 10 minutes. Serve on a bed of vegetables.

∼∼∼∼∼∼∼∼∼∼∼∼

*NOTE: GARLIC CLOVES COOKED IN THE OVEN KEEP VERY WELL IN THE REFRIGERATOR, COVERED WITH OLIVE OIL IN AN AIRTIGHT CONTAINER. THEY CAN BE FLAVORED WITH THYME AND/OR BAY LEAVES.

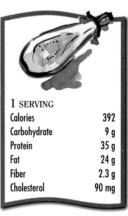

1 SERVING	
Calories	392
Carbohydrate	9 g
Protein	35 g
Fat	24 g
Fiber	2.3 g
Cholesterol	90 mg

SARDINE ROLLS WITH THYME AND PARMESAN

24	fresh sardines	24
1	garlic clove, chopped	1
1	onion, finely chopped	1
1 tbsp	chopped fresh parsley	15 mL
2 tbsp	chopped fresh thyme	30 mL
¼ cup	breadcrumbs	50 mL
½ cup	freshly grated Parmesan cheese	125 mL
½ cup	ricotta cheese	125 mL
1 tbsp	olive oil	15 mL
	salt and freshly ground pepper	

≈ Prepare sardines as shown on page 10.

≈ Preheat oven to 400°F (200°C). In a bowl, mix together garlic, onion, parsley, thyme, breadcrumbs, Parmesan and ricotta cheeses; season with salt and pepper. Place open sardines skin-side-down on a cutting board and season.

≈ Place a heaping teaspoon of cheese filling on the wide end of each sardine. Roll sardines, starting with the wide end and finishing with the tail. Secure with a toothpick.

≈ Lightly oil the bottom of an ovenproof dish and arrange sardines on top; cook 10 to 12 minutes in oven.

4 SERVINGS

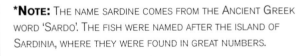

*NOTE: THE NAME SARDINE COMES FROM THE ANCIENT GREEK WORD 'SARDO'. THE FISH WERE NAMED AFTER THE ISLAND OF SARDINIA, WHERE THEY WERE FOUND IN GREAT NUMBERS.

Mix together garlic, onion, parsley, thyme, breadcrumbs, Parmesan and ricotta cheeses.

Place a heaping teaspoon of cheese filling on the wide end of each sardine.

Roll carefully and secure with a toothpick.

1 SERVING	
Calories	364
Carbohydrate	8 g
Protein	29 g
Fat	24 g
Fiber	0.4 g
Cholesterol	90 mg

IN THE OVEN

209

COD BRANDADE WITH GARLIC TOAST

2 lbs	salted cod	1 kg
1⅔ cups	olive oil	400 mL
½ cup	2% milk	125 mL
½ cup	heavy cream (35% MF)	125 mL
1	French bread, sliced	1
2	garlic cloves, halved	2
	salt and white pepper	

～ Soak cod in cold water 12 hours, changing water 2 or 3 times. Cut into cubes and place in saucepan full of cold water; bring to a boil. Reduce heat to medium and cook 10 minutes.

～ Remove cod from saucepan with slotted spoon and drain. Remove skin and bones; break flesh into small pieces.

～ Heat 2 tbsp (30 mL) olive oil in a heavy saucepan. Add cod and cook about 8 minutes over low heat, stirring constantly. Remove from heat and add milk and cream. Season and gradually add remaining olive oil, stirring constantly. When all the oil has been mixed in, the brandade should be smooth and creamy.

～ Preheat oven to 400°F (200°C). Lightly toast slices of French bread and brush with cut garlic cloves.

～ Place brandade in an ovenproof dish and bake 10 minutes. Serve with garlic toast.

4 SERVINGS

*NOTE: BRANDADE IS A SPECIALTY FROM THE FRENCH REGIONS OF LANGUEDOC AND PROVENCE. THE WORD COMES FROM THE PROVENÇAL VERB 'BRANDAR' WHICH MEANS TO STIR.

1 SERVING	
Calories	1,316
Carbohydrate	39 g
Protein	56 g
Fat	104 g
Fiber	1.1 g
Cholesterol	146 mg

*NOTE: AFTER GUTTING THE
FISH, REMOVE THE STRING OF
COAGULATED BLOOD FROM
THE BACKBONE USING THE
POINT OF A KNIFE.

BLUEFISH EN CROÛTE DE SEL

1	whole bluefish, about 4 lbs (1.8 kg), cleaned*	1
2 lbs	coarse salt	1 kg

LEMON AND CHIVES VINAIGRETTE (OPTIONAL)

¼ cup	lemon juice	50 mL
1 tbsp	Meaux mustard	15 mL
1 cup	olive oil	250 mL
2 tbsp	chopped fresh chives	30 mL
	sea salt and freshly ground pepper	

≈ Preheat oven to 425°F (220°C).

≈ Line a cast-iron or ceramic oval dish with a layer of coarse salt. Place bluefish on top and cover with coarse salt.

≈ Cook 45 minutes in oven. Remove from oven and break the crust of salt that has formed on top. Remove skin and fillet the bluefish.

≈ In a bowl, whisk together lemon juice and mustard. Season and add olive oil in thin stream, whisking constantly. Add chopped chives and mix well. Serve vinaigrette with bluefish.

4 SERVINGS

1 SERVING	
Calories	253
Carbohydrate	0 g
Protein	43 g
Fat	9 g
Fiber	0 g
Cholesterol	128 mg

SEAFOOD TURNOVERS WITH BELL PEPPERS ∼

8	filo pastry sheets*	8
½ cup	melted butter	125 mL
8	fresh medium scallops	8
12	medium shrimp, peeled and deveined	12
1	red bell pepper, diced	1
1	yellow bell pepper, diced	1
1	fennel bulb, diced	1
	salt and freshly ground pepper	

∼ Preheat oven to 425°F (220°C).

∼ Place 1 sheet of filo pastry on top of another and brush with melted butter. Fold them in half and brush again with melted butter.

∼ Place 2 scallops and 3 shrimp in the center; season well. Add red pepper, yellow pepper and fennel.

∼ Close the turnover by folding the two sides over the filling and rolling the ends towards the center. Brush the surface with melted butter.

∼ Repeat the operation with the remaining ingredients to make 4 turnovers. Bake 10 to 12 minutes in oven.

4 SERVINGS

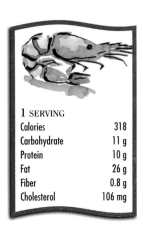

1 SERVING	
Calories	318
Carbohydrate	11 g
Protein	10 g
Fat	26 g
Fiber	0.8 g
Cholesterol	106 mg

Brush sheets of filo pastry with butter and fold in two.

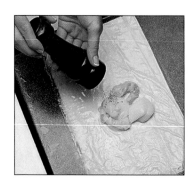

Place 2 scallops and 3 shrimp in the center and season well.

Add fennel and bell peppers.

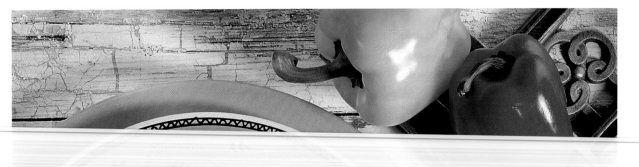

*NOTE: VERY THIN FILO PASTRY IS USED A LOT IN GREEK CUISINE. YOU CAN KEEP IT IN THE REFRIGERATOR 1 MONTH IF THE PACKAGE IS UNOPENED, 3 TO 4 DAYS IF IT IS OPEN. A SEALED PACKAGE WILL KEEP 1 YEAR IN THE FREEZER.

Fold the two sides over the filling.

Roll the ends towards the center.

Brush with melted butter.

COQUILLES ST-JACQUES WITH MASHED POTATOES

3	large potatoes, cubed	3
3 tbsp	butter	45 mL
¼ cup	hot milk	50 mL
1 lb	fresh scallops	450 g
2	dry shallots, finely chopped	2
¾ cup	dry white wine	175 mL
1 cup	fish stock	250 mL
3	fresh parsley sprigs	3
3 tbsp	all-purpose flour	45 mL
¼ cup	heavy cream (35% MF)	50 mL
¾ cup	grated Gruyère cheese	175 mL
	salt and freshly ground pepper	

~ Cook potatoes in a saucepan of salted, boiling water until tender. Drain well. Purée potatoes in a blender or food mill and transfer to bowl. Add 1 tbsp (15 mL) of butter and hot milk, season with salt and pepper and mix well. Cover and keep warm.

~ In a large sauté pan, place scallops, shallots, wine, fish stock and parsley. Cover and bring to a boil over medium heat. Remove from heat. Turn scallops over and let stand 2 minutes.

~ Remove scallops from pan with a slotted spoon and set aside. Continue cooking liquid 6 minutes over high heat; discard parsley. Transfer liquid to a bowl and set aside.

~ Heat remaining butter in saucepan over medium heat. Sprinkle in flour, mix well and add reserved cooking liquid, blending with a whisk. Correct seasoning.

~ Add cream, stir and cook sauce 6 to 8 minutes over low heat. Add scallops and simmer 2 minutes.

~ Fill a pastry bag with mashed potatoes and squeeze potatoes around the edge of each scallop shell. Spoon scallops and sauce into center of shells and top with Gruyère cheese. Broil 3 minutes in oven or until lightly golden.

4 SERVINGS

*NOTE: COQUILLE ST-JACQUES IS THE NAME GIVEN TO THE WHOLE MOLLUSK, INCLUDING THE SHELL, THE SCALLOP, THE MEMBRANE AND THE BEARDS, AS WELL AS THE CORAL. FOR THIS RECIPE, TRY AND FIND SCALLOP SHELLS WHICH ARE OFTEN SOLD SEPARATELY.

1 SERVING	
Calories	389
Carbohydrate	24 g
Protein	26 g
Fat	21 g
Fiber	1.4 g
Cholesterol	100 mg

Fresh Scampi alla Parmigiana

20	large scampi	20
2 tbsp	olive oil	30 mL
2	garlic cloves, finely chopped	2
2 tbsp	chopped fresh parsley	30 mL
¼ cup	freshly grated Parmesan cheese	50 mL
2 tbsp	breadcrumbs	30 mL
	salt and freshly ground pepper	

≈ Preheat oven to 400°F (200°C).

≈ Place scampi shell-side-up on cutting board. Using a knife, cut lengthwise through shell, leaving enough flesh intact to open butterfly-style.

≈ Combine olive oil, garlic, parsley, Parmesan cheese and breadcrumbs. Season scampi and top with cheese mixture. Cook 7 to 8 minutes in oven. Serve with lemon.

4 SERVINGS

***NOTE:** SCAMPI ARE A PARTICULAR KIND OF LARGE SHRIMP THAT ARE NOW QUITE SCARCE AND THEREFORE MUCH PRIZED. IF YOU CANNOT FIND THEM, YOU CAN USE JUMBO SHRIMP FOR THIS RECIPE.

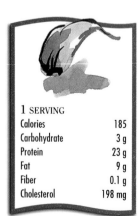

1 SERVING	
Calories	185
Carbohydrate	3 g
Protein	23 g
Fat	9 g
Fiber	0.1 g
Cholesterol	198 mg

*NOTE: ALMONDS ARE VERY NUTRITIOUS. THEY ARE RICH IN FIBER, HAVE NO CHOLESTEROL AND ARE AN EXCELLENT SOURCE OF VITAMIN E AND MAGNESIUM.

PORGY FILLETS WITH ALMONDS

4	porgy fillets, about ⅓ lb (150 g) each, skinned	4
2 tbsp	softened butter	30 mL
1 tbsp	chopped fresh parsley	15 mL
4 tbsp	breadcrumbs	60 mL
½ cup	ground almonds	125 mL
2 tbsp	olive oil	30 mL
2	dry shallots, chopped	2
20	mini zucchini, sliced	20
8 oz	yellow beans, steamed	250 g
	salt and freshly ground pepper	

≈ Preheat oven to 375°F (190°C).

≈ Season porgy fillets. Combine butter, parsley, breadcrumbs and ground almonds. Coat fillets with this mixture and place them in a lightly oiled, ovenproof dish.

≈ Cook fish 10 minutes in oven. Meanwhile, heat oil in a frying pan and sauté shallots 2 minutes.

≈ Add zucchini and continue cooking 3 minutes. Serve porgy fillets with sautéed zucchini and steamed yellow beans.

4 SERVINGS

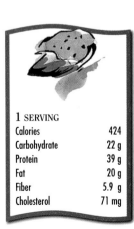

1 SERVING	
Calories	424
Carbohydrate	22 g
Protein	39 g
Fat	20 g
Fiber	5.9 g
Cholesterol	71 mg

*NOTE: Koulibiaca is a Russian pie, traditionally made with cabbage and buckwheat semolina. There have been many adaptations, and now it is prepared with brioche dough or puff pastry.

Cover mushrooms with rice and then salmon.

Cover with sorrel or spinach leaves and hard-boiled egg wedges.

Cover with a layer of puff pastry.

KOULIBIACA

1 lb	fresh salmon, skinned	450 g
¼ lb	sorrel or spinach leaves	115 g
1½ cups	cooked rice	375 mL
1 tbsp	chopped fresh parsley	15 mL
1 tbsp	chopped fresh chives	15 mL
1 tbsp	butter	15 mL
2	dry shallots, chopped	2
½ lb	mushrooms, diced	225 g
1 lb	puff pastry	450 g
2	hard-boiled eggs, quartered	2
1	egg yolk, beaten with 1 tbsp (15 mL) water	1
	fine herb coulis (see recipe page 250)	
	salt and freshly ground pepper	

~ In a large saucepan, bring 8 cups (2 L) water to a boil. Add salmon and cook over medium heat 8 minutes. Remove fish and let cool; flake and set aside. Blanch sorrel or spinach leaves in fish broth 1 minute. Drain well.

~ Combine rice, parsley and chives and set aside.

~ Melt butter in a frying pan over medium-high heat; add shallots and cook 2 minutes. Add mushrooms and cook until all liquid has evaporated. Season and set aside.

~ Preheat oven to 350°F (180°C).

~ Roll out pastry into a rectangle about 8 x 12 inches (20 x 30 cm). Drain mushrooms well and spread them out over pastry, leaving a border of 1 inch (2.5 cm) all around. Cover with rice.

~ Spread salmon on top, then the sorrel or spinach leaves and finally the hard-boiled egg wedges. Moisten the edges of the pastry, and cover completely with another rectangle of pastry, about 10 x 14 inches (25 x 35 cm); pinch edges of 2 rectangles together to seal.

~ Brush surface of pastry with beaten egg yolk and cook in oven 30 to 40 minutes. Serve with fine herb coulis.

4 SERVINGS

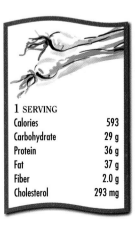

1 SERVING	
Calories	593
Carbohydrate	29 g
Protein	36 g
Fat	37 g
Fiber	2.0 g
Cholesterol	293 mg

Paella Valenciana

16	fresh mussels, washed, scrubbed and bearded	16
1 cup	dry white wine	250 mL
12	fresh clams, scrubbed	12
2 tbsp	olive oil	30 mL
2	onions, chopped	2
2 cups	long-grain rice, rinsed	500 mL
3	tomatoes, peeled, seeded and chopped	3
1	chorizo sausage, sliced	1
1	green bell pepper, halved and sliced	1
3	garlic cloves, chopped	3
2 tbsp	chopped fresh parsley	30 mL
1 tbsp	chopped fresh thyme	15 mL
1	large pinch saffron	1
¼ tsp	Cayenne pepper	1 mL
1 lb	fresh medium shrimp, peeled and deveined	450 g
1 cup	fresh or frozen peas	250 mL
	salt and freshly ground pepper	

≈ Place mussels and wine in a saucepan. Cover and cook over high heat about 8 minutes, or until shells open. Remove with slotted spoon and set aside, discarding any unopened mussels. Cook clams the same way.

≈ Strain cooking liquid through sieve lined with cheesecloth. Add enough water to make 4 cups (1 L) and set aside.

≈ Preheat oven to 350°F (180°C). Heat oil in paella dish or ovenproof frying pan over medium heat. Add onion and rice; cook 4 minutes. Stir in tomatoes, chorizo, green pepper, garlic, parsley, thyme, saffron and Cayenne pepper; season well. Pour in reserved liquid and cook, uncovered, 15 minutes in oven.

≈ Remove from oven and add shrimp, mussels, clams and peas. Return to oven and cook 8 minutes; mix well and serve.

4 SERVINGS

*NOTE: PAELLA IS A TRADITIONAL SPANISH MEAL. ITS NAME DERIVES FROM THE DISH IN WHICH IT IS PREPARED, A 'PAELLERA', WHICH IS A LARGE DEEP FRYING PAN WITH TWO HANDLES.

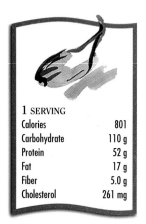

1 SERVING	
Calories	801
Carbohydrate	110 g
Protein	52 g
Fat	17 g
Fiber	5.0 g
Cholesterol	261 mg

MUSSELS AU GRATIN

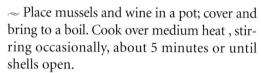

4 lbs	mussels, washed, scrubbed and bearded	1.8 kg
½ cup	dry white wine	125 mL
1 cup	heavy cream (35% MF)	250 mL
1 tbsp	butter	15 mL
1	onion, finely chopped	1
1	garlic clove, finely chopped	1
½ lb	mushrooms, finely chopped	225 g
2 tbsp	chopped fresh basil	30 mL
¼ cup	breadcrumbs	50 mL
	salt and freshly ground pepper	

∼ Place mussels and wine in a pot; cover and bring to a boil. Cook over medium heat , stirring occasionally, about 5 minutes or until shells open.

∼ Remove mussels from shells, discarding any that do not open, and set aside. Strain cooking liquid through a sieve into a saucepan and bring to a boil. Lower heat and add cream; cook until reduced by half and keep warm.

∼ Preheat oven to 400°F (200°C).

∼ Melt butter in sauté pan over high heat. Add onion and cook 3 minutes. Add garlic and mushrooms; season well. Continue cooking 4 minutes over medium heat.

∼ Add mussels and mushroom mixture to sauce; mix well. Add basil and correct seasoning. Transfer to individual ramekins or to a baking dish, sprinkle with breadcrumbs and bake 10 minutes in oven.

4 SERVINGS

*NOTE: 'AU GRATIN' IS A METHOD OF COOKING FISH, MEAT, VEGETABLES AND PASTA WITH A CRUST OF GRATED CHEESE OR BREADCRUMBS THAT IS BROWNED IN THE OVEN. THE CRUST NOT ONLY ENHANCES THE FLAVOR OF THESE DISHES, BUT ALSO PREVENTS THE FOOD FROM DRYING OUT.

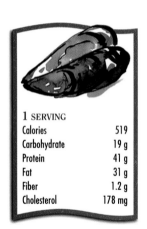

1 SERVING	
Calories	519
Carbohydrate	19 g
Protein	41 g
Fat	31 g
Fiber	1.2 g
Cholesterol	178 mg

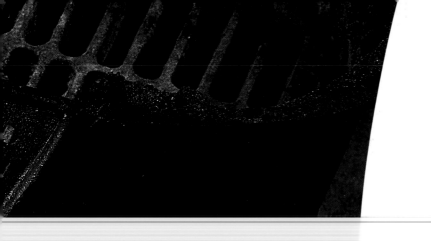

GRILLED

Meals cooked on the barbecue always bring to mind

family get-togethers and summer festivities. But you

don't have to wait for a special occasion to relax and

enjoy the succulent taste of grilled fish and seafood.

Perfumed with fine herbs and sprinkled with olive

oil and lemon juice, the appetizing aromas of the

dishes suggested in this chapter will soon have you

and your family clamoring for a seat at the table.

Whether grilled on the barbecue or in the oven,

the results year round are simply delicious.

BONITO WITH CREAMY POIVRE VERT SAUCE

3 tbsp	olive oil	45 mL
1 tbsp	Dijon mustard	15 mL
2	garlic cloves, blanched and puréed	2
½ tbsp	chopped fresh sage	10 mL
4	bonito steaks, about 6 oz (175 g) each	4
1 tbsp	butter	15 mL
2	dry shallots, chopped	2
1 tbsp	green peppercorns, crushed	15 mL
1 cup	heavy cream (35% MF)	250 mL
	juice of ½ lemon	
	salt and freshly ground pepper	

~ In a bowl, combine olive oil, Dijon mustard, garlic purée, sage and lemon juice. Brush over fish and marinate 1 hour. Season steaks and place on preheated grill over high heat. Grill 5 minutes on each side.

~ Meanwhile, melt butter in a small saucepan and sauté shallots 2 minutes. Add green peppercorns, mix well and stir in cream. Cook over medium heat about 8 minutes or until thickened as desired. Serve fish with green peppercorn sauce.

~ Note: for a spicier sauce, double the amount of crushed green peppercorns.

4 SERVINGS

*NOTE: GREEN PEPPERCORNS, PICKED BEFORE THEY ARE RIPE, ARE SOLD DRIED, IN VINEGAR OR IN BRINE. IF THEY ARE IN BRINE, THEY MUST BE RINSED BEFORE THEY ARE USED.

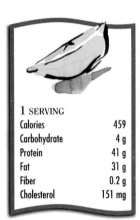

1 SERVING	
Calories	459
Carbohydrate	4 g
Protein	41 g
Fat	31 g
Fiber	0.2 g
Cholesterol	151 mg

*NOTE: BLACK SEA BASS
FEEDS MAINLY ON CRABS AND
SHRIMP. ITS FLESH IS FIRM
AND HAS A DELICATE FLAVOR.

BLACK SEA BASS WITH CITRUS MARINADE

¼ cup	extra virgin olive oil	50 mL
2 tbsp	chopped fresh dill	30 mL
1	4-lb (2 kg) black sea bass, cleaned	1
	juice of 1 lemon	
	juice of 1 lime	
	juice of 1 orange	
	salt and freshly ground pepper	

≈ In a bowl, combine oil, dill, lemon, lime and orange juices. Brush fish with mixture, inside and out. Season well.

≈ Cook fish 35 to 40 minutes on barbecue over medium heat, turning fish several times. Baste frequently.

≈ Serve with citrus fruit marinade.

4 SERVINGS

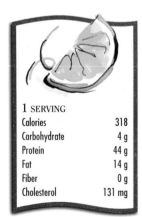

1 SERVING	
Calories	318
Carbohydrate	4 g
Protein	44 g
Fat	14 g
Fiber	0 g
Cholesterol	131 mg

GRILLED SALMON TERIYAKI

~

¼ cup	soy sauce	50 mL
¼ cup	mirin*	50 mL
¼ cup	sake*	50 mL
2 tbsp	honey	30 mL

~ In a shallow dish, combine soy sauce, mirin, sake, honey and oil. Add salmon and marinate 10 minutes.

~ Cook salmon on preheated barbecue over medium heat, 5 minutes on each side, or until

~~~~~~~~~~~~~~~~

*NOTE: SAKE IS A JAPANESE ALCOHOLIC BEVERAGE MADE FROM FERMENTED RICE AND WATER. THERE ARE SEVERAL VARIETIES, INCLUDING 'TOSO' WHICH IS SWEET AND SPICY AND 'SEISHU' WHICH IS OFTEN EXPORTED. 'MIRIN' IS ALSO A KIND OF SAKE, MADE WITH RICE AND DISTILLED ALCOHOL; IT IS USED MAINLY FOR COOKING.

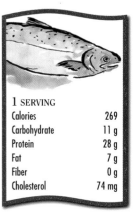

1 SERVING	
Calories	269
Carbohydrate	11 g
Protein	28 g
Fat	7 g
Fiber	0 g
Cholesterol	74 mg

GRILLED MACKEREL WRAPPED IN VINE LEAVES ~

¼ cup	bulgur (cracked wheat)	50 mL
½ cup	chopped fresh parsley	125 mL
¼ cup	chopped fresh mint	50 mL
1	tomato, finely chopped	1
2 tbsp	extra virgin olive oil	30 mL
1⅓ lbs	mackerel fillets, skinned	600 g
16	large grape vine leaves, rinsed	16
	juice of ½ lemon	
	salt and freshly ground pepper	

~ Place bulgur in a bowl, cover with cold water and let stand 1 hour. Drain bulgur, place in bowl and add parsley, mint and tomato; mix well. Add olive oil and lemon juice; season with pepper.

~ Remove any bones from mackerel fillets, and place fish on cutting board. Cover 1 fillet with bulgur mixture and top with a second fillet. Season with salt and pepper and cut into 1 inch (2.5 cm) slices. Repeat with remaining fillets.

~ Wrap each piece in a vine leaf and grill on preheated barbecue over medium heat about 4 minutes on each side. Serve hot or cold.

4 SERVINGS

1 SERVING	
Calories	230
Carbohydrate	4 g
Protein	31 g
Fat	10 g
Fiber	1.9 g
Cholesterol	79 mg

Soak bulgur in water and let stand 1 hour.

Drain bulgur and add parsley, mint and tomato.

Cover 1 mackerel fillet with bulgur mixture.

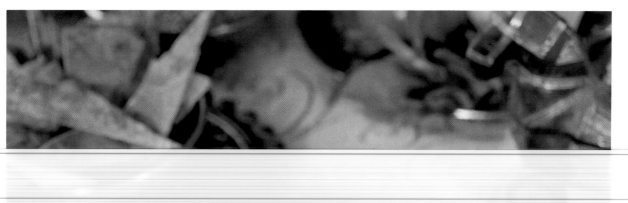

~~~~~~~~~~~~~~~~

*NOTE: VINE LEAVES
ENHANCE THE FLAVOR OF
THE MACKEREL AND KEEP
THE JUICES INSIDE AS THE
FILLETS ARE BEING COOKED.

Top with a second fillet.

Cut into 1-inch (2.5 cm) slices.

Wrap each slice in a vine leaf.

231

BALINESE SEAFOOD SATAY

1	red chili pepper, seeded and finely chopped	1
2 tbsp	brown sugar	30 mL
3	garlic cloves	3
4	dry shallots	4
1	2-inch (5 cm) piece fresh ginger, peeled	1
1	2-inch (5 cm) piece fresh turmeric, peeled	1
2	tomatoes, peeled, seeded and chopped	2
2 tbsp	vegetable oil	30 mL
½ lb	skinned red snapper fillets	225 g
½ lb	shrimp, peeled and deveined	225 g
1 cup	freshly grated coconut	250 mL
24	lemon grass stalks or bamboo skewers, soaked in water	24
	sea salt	

∼ Place chili pepper, brown sugar, garlic, shallots, ginger, turmeric, tomatoes and vegetable oil in blender and purée.

∼ In a food processor, finely chop red snapper and shrimp. Add grated coconut and spicy purée; mix well and season with salt.

∼ Place about 3 tbsp (45 mL) of mixture around each lemon grass stalk or bamboo skewer and press firmly to hold it in place.

∼ Grill satay brochettes on very hot, oiled barbecue about 2 minutes on each side, or until golden brown.

4 SERVINGS

*NOTE: THIS INDONESIAN SPECIALTY CAN BE SERVED AT ANY HOUR OF THE DAY, AS A SNACK, AN APPETIZER OR A MAIN DISH.

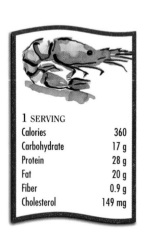

1 SERVING	
Calories	360
Carbohydrate	17 g
Protein	28 g
Fat	20 g
Fiber	0.9 g
Cholesterol	149 mg

SCALLOPS AND SHRIMP ON THE GRILL

3 tbsp	extra virgin olive oil	45 mL
1 tbsp	chopped fresh rosemary	15 mL
1 tbsp	chopped fresh parsley	15 mL
12	fresh scallops	12
8	large fresh shrimp, peeled and deveined	8
4	marinated artichoke hearts	4
	juice and zest of 1 lemon	
	wooden skewers	
	sea salt and freshly ground pepper	

~ In a bowl, combine olive oil, rosemary, parsley, lemon juice and zest. Add scallops and shrimp and let marinate 30 minutes.

~ Thread scallops and shrimp onto skewers.* (Set marinade aside.) Season seafood and grill on preheated barbecue 3 minutes on each side.

~ Serve scallops and shrimp with artichoke hearts, sprinkled with reserved marinade.

4 SERVINGS

*NOTE: WOODEN SKEWERS SHOULD BE SOAKED IN WATER FOR HALF AN HOUR BEFORE THEY ARE USED SO THAT THEY DON'T BURN ON THE GRILL.

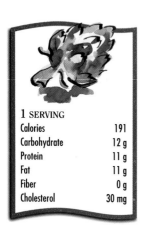

1 SERVING	
Calories	191
Carbohydrate	12 g
Protein	11 g
Fat	11 g
Fiber	0 g
Cholesterol	30 mg

*NOTE: SALMON TROUT IS A
VARIETY OF TROUT,THAT LIVES
IN LAKES AND FAST-FLOWING
STREAMS. IT FEEDS LARGELY
ON SHELLFISH, WHICH TURNS
ITS FLESH PINK; HENCE
THE NAME.

SALMON TROUT WITH GARLIC VINAIGRETTE ∼

3 tbsp	extra virgin olive oil	45 mL
1 tbsp	red wine vinegar	15 mL
1 tsp	Dijon mustard	5 mL
2	garlic cloves, finely chopped	2
2	Italian tomatoes, seeded and very thinly sliced	2
4	slices salmon trout fillet, about ⅓ lb (150 g) each	4
	salt and freshly ground pepper	

∼ Combine olive oil, vinegar, mustard, garlic and tomato slices. Set aside.

∼ Season trout and cook on preheated barbecue about 2 minutes on each side over medium heat.

∼ Serve with the garlic vinaigrette, new potatoes and steamed leeks, if desired.

4 SERVINGS

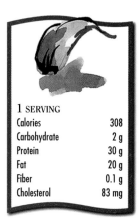

1 SERVING	
Calories	308
Carbohydrate	2 g
Protein	30 g
Fat	20 g
Fiber	0.1 g
Cholesterol	83 mg

SPICY RED SNAPPER GRILLED IN BANANA LEAVES ≈

2	red chili peppers, seeded	2
3	garlic cloves	3
5	dry shallots	5
1	2-inch (5 cm) piece of fresh ginger, peeled	1
1	2-inch (5 cm) piece of fresh turmeric, peeled	1
1 tsp	coriander seeds	5 mL
2	tomatoes, peeled and seeded	2
½ cup	chicken stock	125 mL
3 tbsp	peanut oil	45 mL
1⅓ lbs	red snapper fillets, cut in 8 pieces	600 g
4	banana leaves,* cut in 9-inch (20 cm) squares	4

≈ Place chili peppers, garlic cloves, shallots, ginger, turmeric, coriander seeds, tomatoes, chicken stock and oil in blender and purée.

≈ Place red snapper pieces in a baking dish and pour in spicy purée; let marinate 2 hours in the refrigerator.

≈ To soften banana leaves, plunge into boiling water for 2 minutes. Place 2 pieces of red snapper, one on top of the other, on each banana leaf. Fold leaf over to form a package. Tie with string and grill on pre-heated barbecue 5 to 6 minutes on each side.

4 SERVINGS

~~~~~~~~~~~~~~~~~~~~~~~~~~~~~~~~~~

*NOTE: BANANA LEAVES CAN BE FOUND IN CERTAIN SPECIALTY STORES (CARIBBEAN, AFRICAN, SOUTH-AMERICAN AND ASIAN). THEY SHOULD BE KEPT IN THE FREEZER UNTIL READY TO USE.

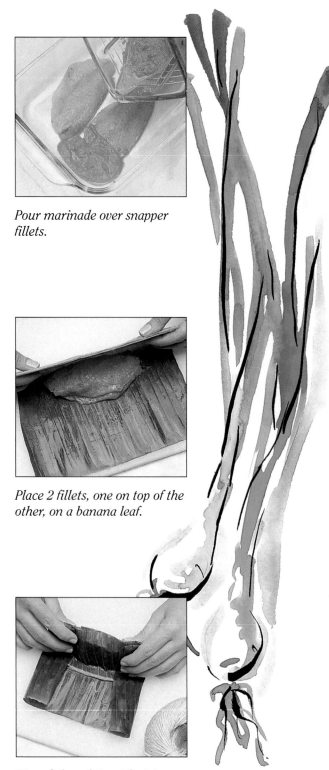

Pour marinade over snapper fillets.

Place 2 fillets, one on top of the other, on a banana leaf.

Wrap fish and tie with string.

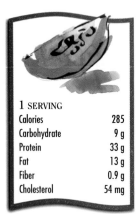

1 SERVING	
Calories	285
Carbohydrate	9 g
Protein	33 g
Fat	13 g
Fiber	0.9 g
Cholesterol	54 mg

SALMON TOURNEDOS WITH HERB BUTTER

4	salmon steaks, about 6 oz (175 g) each	4
¼ cup	unsalted butter, softened	50 mL
2	dry shallots, chopped	2
2 tbsp	wholegrain mustard	30 mL
2 tbsp	chopped fresh parsley	30 mL
1 tbsp	chopped fresh dill	15 mL
	salt and freshly ground pepper	

≈ Prepare salmon tournedos as shown on page 9.

≈ Melt 1 tbsp (15 mL) butter in a small saucepan. Add shallots and sauté 2 minutes. Add mustard and mix well. Stir in remaining butter with a whisk until smooth. Add parsley and dill and keep warm over low heat. If sauce separates, whisk again just before serving.

≈ Season salmon tournedos and cook on preheated barbecue 3 to 4 minutes on each side, or until cooked as desired. Serve with herb butter and fresh asparagus.

4 SERVINGS

*NOTE: DILL LOSES SOME OF ITS FLAVOR WHEN COOKED. IT IS BEST TO ADD IT AT THE LAST MINUTE.

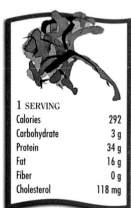

1 SERVING	
Calories	292
Carbohydrate	3 g
Protein	34 g
Fat	16 g
Fiber	0 g
Cholesterol	118 mg

*NOTE: TO CRUSH BLACK PEPPERCORNS, PLACE IN A THICK PLASTIC BAG AND PRESS DOWN ON THEM WITH A SMALL SAUCEPAN OR OTHER HEAVY OBJECT.

SICILIAN TUNA PEPPER STEAKS

4	fresh tuna steaks, about 6 oz (175 g) each	4
3 tbsp	crushed black peppercorns	45 mL
2 tbsp	chopped fresh oregano	30 mL
½ cup	extra virgin olive oil	125 mL
4	red tomatoes, cut in wedges	4
4	yellow tomatoes, cut in wedges	4
	juice of 2 lemons	
	salt	
	fresh oregano for garnish	

~ Preheat barbecue; grill should be very hot so that steaks do not stick to it. Coat tuna steaks with crushed peppercorns and set aside.

~ With a fork, mix together lemon juice and chopped oregano. Gradually whisk in olive oil and set vinaigrette aside.

~ Distribute tomato wedges among 4 individual plates.

~ Season tuna with salt and grill over high heat about 2 minutes on each side. Place 1 steak in the center of each plate, sprinkle with vinaigrette and garnish with fresh oregano. Serve with pasta, if desired.

4 SERVINGS

1 SERVING	
Calories	523
Carbohydrate	18 g
Protein	43 g
Fat	31 g
Fiber	3.4 g
Cholesterol	85 mg

STRIPED BASS WITH TAPENADE AND ARTICHOKES

1 tbsp	balsamic vinegar	15 mL
3 tbsp	extra virgin olive oil	45 mL
1	garlic clove, chopped	1
6	artichoke hearts, quartered	6
3	small red onions, sliced	3
4	striped bass filets, about ⅓ lb (150 g) each, unskinned	4
16	fresh oregano leaves	16
4 tbsp	tapenade*	60 mL
	sea salt and freshly ground pepper	

≈ In a bowl, mix together balsamic vinegar, olive oil and garlic. Add artichoke hearts and onions; season and let marinate 30 minutes.

≈ Meanwhile, brush striped bass fillets with a bit of olive oil and season with salt and pepper. Cook on a very hot grill, 3 minutes on each side.

≈ Stir oregano into marinated artichokes. Cut each bass fillet in half; serve with marinated artichokes and tapenade.

4 SERVINGS

*NOTE: A FRENCH CONDIMENT FROM THE PROVENCE REGION, TAPENADE IS PREPARED WITH PITTED BLACK OLIVES, DESALTED ANCHOVIES AND CAPERS, POUNDED IN A MORTAR AND SEASONED WITH LEMON JUICE AND OLIVE OIL.

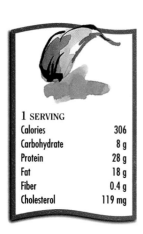

1 SERVING	
Calories	306
Carbohydrate	8 g
Protein	28 g
Fat	18 g
Fiber	0.4 g
Cholesterol	119 mg

SCAMPI KEBABS WITH THYME AND GARLIC ≈

¼ cup	extra virgin olive oil	50 mL
12	garlic cloves, blanched	12
1 tbsp	chopped fresh thyme	15 mL
24	large scampi, peeled and deveined	24
1	pinch of paprika	1
	juice of 1 lemon	
	small bamboo skewers*	
	salt and freshly ground pepper	

≈ In a bowl, mix together lemon juice, olive oil, garlic and thyme. Add scampi and marinate 30 minutes.

≈ Alternate the scampi and garlic cloves on skewers. Season well and sprinkle with paprika.

≈ Cook 6 minutes on a preheated grill, turning once during cooking and basting frequently with marinade. Serve immediately.

4 SERVINGS

*NOTE: BAMBOO SKEWERS SHOULD BE SOAKED FOR HALF AN HOUR IN COLD WATER BEFORE THEY ARE USED. OTHERWISE THEY MAY BURN ON THE GRILL.

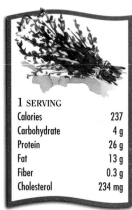

1 SERVING	
Calories	237
Carbohydrate	4 g
Protein	26 g
Fat	13 g
Fiber	0.3 g
Cholesterol	234 mg

SEASONING; IT IS A BIT
SALTIER AND ENHANCES FISH
ESPECIALLY WELL. THE
DARKER VERSION IS MADE
WITH MOLASSES AND IS AGED
LONGER. USED IN COOKING, IT
HAS A STRONGER FLAVOR.

BARBECUED SWEET AND SOUR HALIBUT

4	halibut steaks, about 6 oz (175 g) each	4
3 tbsp	peanut oil	45 mL
1 tbsp	sesame oil	15 mL
2 tbsp	soy sauce*	30 mL
2 tbsp	honey	30 mL
3	garlic cloves, finely chopped	3
¼ cup	chicken stock	50 mL
	juice of ½ lemon	
	freshly ground pepper	

～ Place halibut steaks in a roasting pan and season with pepper. In a bowl, mix together peanut oil, sesame oil, soy sauce, honey, garlic, chicken stock and lemon juice.

～ Pour mixture over fish and marinate 1 hour. Turn steaks over and marinate 1 hour more.

～ Grill fish on preheated barbecue 6 to 7 minutes on each side, or adjust time depending on thickness. Baste frequently during cooking.

～ Serve fish with vegetable rice and zucchini, if desired.

4 SERVINGS

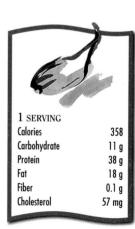

1 SERVING	
Calories	358
Carbohydrate	11 g
Protein	38 g
Fat	18 g
Fiber	0.1 g
Cholesterol	57 mg

TROUT STUFFED WITH PECORINO SPINACH PESTO

4	small whole trout, about ½ lb (225 g) each	4
1 tbsp	butter	15 mL
2 cups	coarsely chopped fresh spinach	500 mL
1 cup	ricotta cheese	250 mL
¼ cup	Pecorino cheese	50 mL
¾ cup	fresh breadcrumbs	175 mL
½ cup	pine nuts, toasted and chopped	125 mL
2 tbsp	olive oil	30 mL
	juice of 1 lemon	
	salt and freshly ground pepper	

≈ Prepare trout as shown on page 7. Melt butter in a frying pan and sauté spinach 2 minutes. Remove from heat and add ricotta cheese; mix well. Stir in Pecorino cheese, breadcrumbs and pine nuts.

≈ Season cavity of each trout and fill with spinach and cheese mixture. Tie trout with string and brush with olive oil.

≈ Grill fish on preheated barbecue 10 minutes, or adjust time depending on size, turning fish once and basting with lemon juice during cooking. Serve immediately.

4 SERVINGS

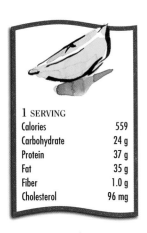

1 SERVING	
Calories	559
Carbohydrate	24 g
Protein	37 g
Fat	35 g
Fiber	1.0 g
Cholesterol	96 mg

Sauté spinach 2 minutes.

Add ricotta and mix well.

Stir in Pecorino, breadcrumbs and pine nuts.

*NOTE: SO THAT THE FILLING STAYS IN THE ABDOMINAL CAVITY OF THE FISH, ROUGHLY SEW THE OPENING SHUT WITH A TRUSSING NEEDLE AND SOME STRING.

Stuff trout with spinach and cheese mixture.

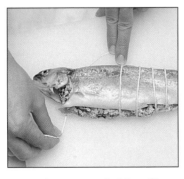

Tie with string to hold stuffing in place.

Brush with olive oil before grilling.

GRILLED SWORDFISH WITH SUN-DRIED TOMATO SAUCE

4 tbsp	olive oil	60 mL
2 tbsp	chopped fresh thyme	30 mL
2	bay leaves	2
4	slices swordfish fillet, about 6 oz (175 g) each	4
2	dry shallots, chopped	2
½ cup	fish stock	125 mL
6	large tomatoes, peeled, seeded and chopped	6
½ cup	sun-dried tomatoes, chopped	125 mL
½	Jamaican hot pepper, seeded and finely chopped	½
	zest and juice of 1 lime	
	salt	

≈ In a baking dish, combine 3 tbsp (45 mL) olive oil, thyme, bay leaves, lime zest and juice. Add swordfish and marinate 1 hour.

≈ Meanwhile, prepare the sauce: heat 1 tbsp (15 mL) olive oil in a saucepan; add shallots and sauté 2 minutes. Add fish stock and continue cooking 2 minutes over medium heat. Add fresh tomatoes and season well.

≈ Add sun-dried tomatoes and hot pepper; cook 15 minutes over medium heat.

≈ Season swordfish and cook on preheated barbecue 6 to 7 minutes on each side. Serve with tomato sauce.

4 SERVINGS

≈≈≈≈≈≈≈≈≈≈≈≈≈≈≈≈≈≈≈≈≈≈≈

*NOTE: TOMATOES KEPT AT ROOM TEMPERATURE ARE MUCH MORE FLAVORFUL THAN THOSE KEPT IN THE REFRIGERATOR. ONE MEDIUM-SIZED TOMATO HAS ALMOST HALF THE DAILY RECOMMENDED DOSE OF VITAMIN C.

1 SERVING	
Calories	387
Carbohydrate	15 g
Protein	39 g
Fat	19 g
Fiber	1.6 g
Cholesterol	70 mg

GRILLED

247

TURBOT, ZUCCHINI AND EGGPLANT KEBABS

1⅓ lbs	**turbot fillets**	**600 g**
3	**small zucchini, sliced**	**3**
1	**medium eggplant,* cubed**	**1**
2	**garlic cloves, finely chopped**	**2**
1 tsp	**chopped fresh thyme**	**5 mL**
½ tsp	**fennel seeds**	**2 mL**
½ tsp	**coriander seeds**	**2 mL**
½ cup	**olive oil**	**125 mL**
	zest of 1 lemon, finely chopped	
	juice of 1 lemon	
	small wooden skewers	
	sea salt and freshly ground pepper	

≈ Cut turbot fillets into long thin slices. Cut each slice into 2½ inch (6 cm) pieces.

≈ Roll up each slice and string onto wooden skewers, alternating with zucchini slices and eggplant cubes.

≈ In a bowl, mix together garlic, lemon zest and juice, thyme, fennel seeds, coriander seeds and olive oil. Season with salt and pepper. Brush kebabs with marinade and refrigerate 1 hour, turning once.

≈ Cook kebabs on preheated barbecue about 4 minutes on each side, basting evenly with marinade. Serve with cherry tomatoes and green salad.

4 SERVINGS

*NOTE: AFTER CUTTING THE EGGPLANT INTO CUBES, SPRINKLE THE FLESH WITH COARSE SALT AND LET STAND FOR 30 MINUTES. RINSE WITH COLD WATER, DRAIN AND PAT DRY WITH PAPER TOWELS. THIS WILL TAKE AWAY SOME OF ITS BITTER TASTE AND STOP IT FROM ABSORBING TOO MUCH GREASE DURING COOKING.

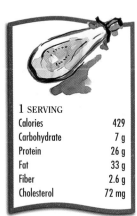

1 SERVING	
Calories	429
Carbohydrate	7 g
Protein	26 g
Fat	33 g
Fiber	2.6 g
Cholesterol	72 mg

*NOTE: CHERVIL IS ORIGINALLY FROM RUSSIA, WHERE IT GROWS WILD, AND WAS INTRODUCED TO THE REST OF EUROPE BY THE ROMANS.

PORGY FILLETS WITH GOAT CHEESE CHERVIL COULIS

1 cup	chicken stock	250 mL
1 cup	chopped fresh chervil	250 mL
1 cup	light cream (15% MF)	250 mL
¼ lb	fresh goat cheese	115 g
4	unskinned porgy fillets, about ⅓ lb (150 g) each	4
2 tbsp	olive oil	30 mL
	juice of ½ lime	
	sea salt and freshly ground pepper	

≈ In a saucepan, bring chicken stock to a boil. Add chervil and blanch 1 minute. Transfer stock and chervil to a blender and purée; add cream. Season and return to saucepan. Add goat cheese and cook over low heat, stirring constantly until cheese melts; keep warm.

≈ Make small incisions in skin of porgy fillets. Brush with olive oil and season with salt and pepper. Cook on very hot grill about 3 minutes on each side; sprinkling with lime juice during cooking.

≈ Serve porgy fillets over goat cheese and chervil purée. Garnish with fresh chervil, if desired.

4 SERVINGS

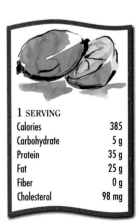

1 SERVING	
Calories	385
Carbohydrate	5 g
Protein	35 g
Fat	25 g
Fiber	0 g
Cholesterol	98 mg

MAYONNAISE

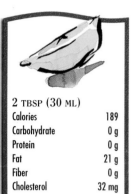

2	egg yolks	2
1 tbsp	Dijon mustard	15 mL
1¼ cups	olive oil	300 mL
2 tsp	wine vinegar	10 mL
	juice of ½ lemon	
	salt and freshly ground pepper	

∾ With a whisk, beat together egg yolks and mustard; season to taste. Add olive oil in a thin stream, whisking constantly.

∾ When mixture starts to thicken, add vinegar and mix well. Add remaining olive oil and lemon juice. Correct seasoning and keep refrigerated.

2 TBSP (30 ML)

Calories	189
Carbohydrate	0 g
Protein	0 g
Fat	21 g
Fiber	0 g
Cholesterol	32 mg

HERB MAYONNAISE

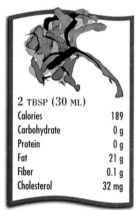

1	recipe mayonnaise (see above)	1
1 tsp	chopped fresh dill	5 mL
1 tbsp	chopped fresh chives	15 mL
1 tbsp	chopped fresh parsley	15 mL
	freshly ground pepper	

∾ Mix together mayonnaise and fine herbs; season with pepper and keep refrigerated until ready to use.

2 TBSP (30 ML)

Calories	189
Carbohydrate	0 g
Protein	0 g
Fat	21 g
Fiber	0.1 g
Cholesterol	32 mg

FINE HERB COULIS

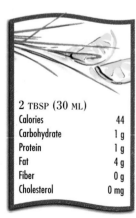

4 tbsp	chopped fresh dill	60 mL
½ cup	chopped fresh chives	125 mL
½ cup	chopped fresh parsley	125 mL
½ cup	chopped fresh chervil	125 mL
1 cup	chicken stock, heated	250 mL
3 tbsp	extra virgin olive oil	45 mL
	salt and freshly ground pepper	

∾ Place dill, chives, parsley, chervil and chicken stock in blender or food processor and purée.

∾ Gradually add olive oil in a thin stream and continue blending. Season and serve hot or at room temperature.

2 TBSP (30 ML)

Calories	44
Carbohydrate	1 g
Protein	1 g
Fat	4 g
Fiber	0 g
Cholesterol	0 mg

MISO AND TAHINI SAUCE

2 tbsp	chopped ginger	30 mL
2 tbsp	rice vinegar	30 mL
½ cup	tahini	125 mL
½ cup	miso	125 mL
	freshly ground pepper	

≈ Mix together ginger, vinegar and tahini. Stir in miso; add enough water to give sauce desired consistency.

≈ Season with pepper and serve sauce with grilled or steamed fish.

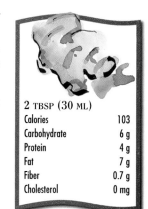

2 TBSP (30 ML)	
Calories	103
Carbohydrate	6 g
Protein	4 g
Fat	7 g
Fiber	0.7 g
Cholesterol	0 mg

FISH STOCK

2 lbs	fish bones	1 kg
2	onions, chopped	2
2	celery stalks	2
¼ lb	mushrooms, sliced	115 g
2	fresh thyme sprigs	2
2	fresh parsley sprigs	2
2	bay leaves	2
	juice of ½ lemon	
	freshly ground pepper	

≈ Rinse fish bones under cold running water and place in a large saucepan. Add onions, celery and mushrooms. Cover with water and bring to a boil. Skim and reduce heat to medium.

≈ Add thyme, parsley, bay leaves, lemon juice and pepper to taste. Cook, uncovered, about 30 minutes. Strain through a sieve lined with cheesecloth.

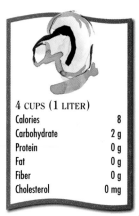

4 CUPS (1 LITER)	
Calories	8
Carbohydrate	2 g
Protein	0 g
Fat	0 g
Fiber	0 g
Cholesterol	0 mg

CREAMY FISH SAUCE

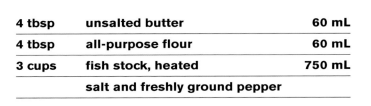

4 tbsp	unsalted butter	60 mL
4 tbsp	all-purpose flour	60 mL
3 cups	fish stock, heated	750 mL
	salt and freshly ground pepper	

≈ Melt butter in saucepan over medium heat. Stir in flour and cook 1 minute over low heat. Pour in stock, season and mix well. Cook over low heat until sauce becomes thick and creamy.

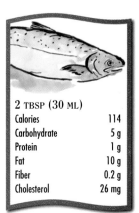

2 TBSP (30 ML)	
Calories	114
Carbohydrate	5 g
Protein	1 g
Fat	10 g
Fiber	0.2 g
Cholesterol	26 mg

DASHI (JAPANESE SOUP STOCK) ≈

8 CUPS (2 LITERS)

Calories	0
Carbohydrate	0 g
Protein	0 g
Fat	0 g
Fiber	0 g
Cholesterol	0 mg

8 cups	water	2 L
⅓ oz	dried bonito flakes	10 g
½	kombu seaweed	½

≈ In a large saucepan, bring water to a boil. Add bonito flakes and kombu seaweed. Cook over medium heat a few seconds, or until bonito flakes sink to the bottom. Strain through cheesecloth.

BASIL OIL ≈

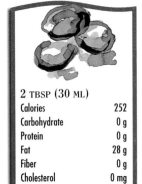

2 TBSP (30 ML)

Calories	252
Carbohydrate	0 g
Protein	0 g
Fat	28 g
Fiber	0 g
Cholesterol	0 mg

2 cups	olive oil	500 mL
2 cups	fresh basil leaves	500 mL

≈ Pour olive oil into a blender or food processor; add basil and purée. Transfer to a glass or ceramic jar and let stand 24 hours.

≈ Strain, making sure to recuperate as much oil as possible, and keep in a cool place until ready to use. This oil is wonderful with salads and grilled fish.

BEURRE BLANC ≈

2 TBSP (30 ML)

Calories	45
Carbohydrate	0 g
Protein	0 g
Fat	5 g
Fiber	0 g
Cholesterol	13 mg

½ lb	cold unsalted butter	225 g
2	dry shallots, chopped	2
	juice of 1 lime	
	salt and freshly ground pepper	

≈ Melt 1 tbsp (15 mL) of butter in pan and sauté shallots 2 minutes. Add lime juice and simmer to thicken. Add the rest of the butter, bit by bit, whisking constantly over low heat. Season with salt and pepper. The sauce should become creamy.

≈ Keep warm over low heat until ready to use. If necessary, whisk lightly just before serving.

HOLLANDAISE SAUCE

2	egg yolks	2
1 tbsp	cold water	15 mL
¾ cup	melted clarified butter	175 mL
	lemon juice	
	salt and freshly ground pepper	

~ Beat egg yolks with water in a stainless steel bowl. Season with salt and pepper and place bowl over a saucepan of simmering water.

~ Add butter, whisking constantly, until sauce is thick and creamy. Add lemon juice to taste and correct seasoning.

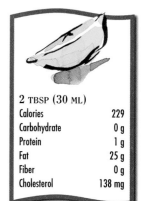

2 TBSP (30 ML)	
Calories	229
Carbohydrate	0 g
Protein	1 g
Fat	25 g
Fiber	0 g
Cholesterol	138 mg

TARTAR SAUCE

1	recipe mayonnaise (see recipe p. 250)	1
1	dry shallot, chopped	1
1 tbsp	chopped fresh parsley	15 mL
2 tbsp	chopped fresh chives	30 mL
2 tbsp	chopped capers	30 mL
4 tbsp	chopped dill pickle	60 mL
	freshly ground pepper	

~ Mix together all ingredients and refrigerate until ready to use.

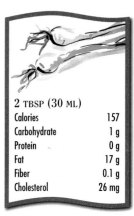

2 TBSP (30 ML)	
Calories	157
Carbohydrate	1 g
Protein	0 g
Fat	17 g
Fiber	0.1 g
Cholesterol	26 mg

COCKTAIL SAUCE

1	recipe mayonnaise (see recipe p. 250)	1
6 tbsp	chili sauce	90 mL
2 tbsp	horseradish	30 mL
2 tbsp	lemon juice	30 mL
	salt and freshly ground pepper	

~ Combine mayonnaise, chili sauce and horseradish; mix well. Add lemon juice and season with salt and pepper. Chill before serving.

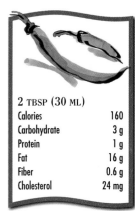

2 TBSP (30 ML)	
Calories	160
Carbohydrate	3 g
Protein	1 g
Fat	16 g
Fiber	0.6 g
Cholesterol	24 mg

INDEX

BLUEFISH
Bluefish en Croûte de Sel *211*
Bluefish Fillets with Tomatillo
  Sauce *168*
Poached Boston Bluefish *133*

BONITO
Bonito with Chinese Vegetables *104*
Bonito with Creamy Poivre Vert
  Sauce *226*
Nigiri-Sushi *62*
Shrimp, Fish and Vegetable
  Tempura *76*

CARP
Japanese Miso Soup with Carp and
  Shiitake Mushrooms *42*
Stir-Fried Carp with Snow Peas *155*

CLAMS
Clam Quiche with Pancetta *204*
Clams Marinara *110*
New England Clam Chowder *49*
Paella Valenciana *220*
Saffron Seafood Stew *178*
Seafood and Saffron Soup *34*
Spicy Clam Fritters with Herb
  Mayonnaise *91*

COD
Cod Brandade with Garlic Toast *210*
Fish and Seafood Pie *198*
Fish and Vegetable Chips *90*
Fresh Cod à la Dijonnaise *122*
Fritto Misto di Mare *93*
Salted Cod à la Créole *132*
Taramasalata *59*

CRAB
Chinese Fish and Seafood Stir-
  Fry *172*
Crab Spring Rolls with Sweet and
  Sour Sauce *88*
Curried Blue Crabs *108*
Deep-Fried Soft-Shelled Crabs *79*
Fish and Seafood Pie *198*
Maki-Sushi *60*
Red Snapper and Spinach
  Wontons *82*
Saffron Seafood Stew *178*
Seafood Gumbo *39*

CRAYFISH
Mediterranean Bouillabaisse *44*

EEL
Eel à la Provençale *153*
Eel Matelote *140*

GROUPER
Grouper Pot-au-feu *120*
Grouper Veracruz *190*

GURNARDS
Mediterranean Bouillabaisse *44*

HADDOCK
Bengali Curry with Haddock *180*
Fresh Cilantro Ceviche *64*
Haddock with Nuoc Cham
  Sauce *147*
Lobster and Haddock with Tarragon
  Sauce *130*
Mexican Escabèche with Orange *25*
Warm Haddock Salad with Bell
  Peppers *28*

HALIBUT
Barbecued Sweet and Sour
  Halibut *243*
Braised Halibut with Sesame and
  Ginger *193*
Halibut and Fresh Fennel Soup *38*
Poached Halibut with Fresh
  Vegetables *128*

HERRING
Marinated Herring and Beet
  Salad *23*

LOBSTER
Lobster and Haddock with Tarragon
  Sauce *130*
Lobster and Scallop Salad with Basil
  Oil *31*
Lobster Bisque *50*
Pike Quenelles with Lobster
  Bisque *127*
Poached Lobster with Lemon Garlic
  Butter *136*

MACKEREL
Crispy Fried Mackerel and
  Sardines *86*
Grilled Mackerel Wrapped in Vine
  Leaves *230*
Sashimi *72*

MONKFISH
Chinese Fish and Seafood Stir-
  Fry *172*
Monkfish and Potato Fricassée *195*
Monkfish Medaillons with Kale
  en Papillote *200*
Monkfish Paprikache *182*

MUSSELS

Mussels au Gratin **222**
Mussels in Creamy White Wine
　　Sauce **100**
Mussels with Orange-Coriander
　　Sauce **113**
Paella Valenciana **220**
Saffron Seafood Stew **178**
Seafood and Saffron Soup **34**
Vichyssoise with Mussels **40**

OCTOPUS

Octopus Salad with Kalamata
　　Olives **30**

OYSTERS

Creamy Oyster and Spinach
　　Soup **48**
Fresh Oyster and Spinach Salad **24**
Golden Fried Oysters with Tartar
　　Sauce **81**

PIKE

Pike Quenelles with Lobster
　　Bisque **127**

POMPANO

Blackened Cajun Pompano **171**
Pompano with Vegetables and
　　Roasted Garlic **207**

PORGY

Fillet of Porgy with Oyster
　　Mushrooms **111**
Porgies with Fennel **117**
Porgy à la Nage **139**
Porgy Fillets with Almonds **217**
Porgy Fillets with Goat Cheese
　　Chervil Coulis **249**

RED MULLETS

Mediterranean Bouillabaisse **44**
Red Mullet in Grapefruit Salsa **206**
Red Mullet with Mushroom and
　　Thyme Sauce **161**

RED SNAPPER

Balinese Seafood Satay **232**
Red Snapper and Spinach
　　Wontons **82**
Red Snapper with Capers and
　　Olives **112**
Red Snapper with Marinated
　　Peppers **144**
Singapore Seafood Soup with
　　Coconut **52**
Singapore Tea-Smoked Red
　　Snapper **66**
Spicy Red Snapper Grilled in Banana
　　Leaves **236**

SALMON

Gravlax **58**
Grilled Salmon Teriyaki **229**
Japanese Salmon and Tofu Balls **84**
Koulibiaca **219**
Maki-Sushi **60**
Poached Salmon and Asparagus
　　Salad **26**
Poached Salmon with Vegetable
　　Julienne **129**
Salmon and Goat Cheese Rolls with
　　Beurre Blanc **114**
Salmon and Scallop Tartare with
　　Chervil **69**
Salmon Croquettes with
　　Almonds **94**
Salmon Steaks with Endive and Basil
　　Sauce **156**
Salmon Tournedos with Herb
　　Butter **238**
Salmon with Hazelnuts and
　　Watercress **165**
Sashimi **72**
Smoked Salmon Blinis **70**
Smoked Salmon Florentine **73**
Smoked Salmon Mousse
　　Canapés **68**
Whole Poached Baby Salmon **135**

SALMON TROUT (SEE TROUT)

SARDINES

Crispy Fried Mackerel and
　　Sardines **86**
Sardine Rolls with Thyme and
　　Parmesan **208**

SAUCES

Basil Oil **252**
Beurre Blanc **252**
Cocktail Sauce **253**
Creamy Fish Sauce **251**
Dashi (Japanese Soup Stock) **252**
Fine Herb Coulis **250**
Fish Stock **251**
Herb Mayonnaise **250**
Hollandaise Sauce **253**
Mayonnaise **250**
Miso and Tahini Sauce **251**
Tartar Sauce **253**

SCALLOPS

Bay Scallops with Fresh Tomatoes
　　and Chives **103**
Coquilles St-Jacques with Mashed
　　Potatoes **215**
Fish and Seafood Pie **198**
Fritto Misto di Mare **93**
Lobster and Scallop Salad with Basil
　　Oil **31**
Madras Curry Scallops **188**
Salmon and Scallop Tartare with
　　Chervil **69**
Scallop Carpaccio with Artichokes
　　and Zucchini **56**
Scallops and Shrimp on the
　　Grill **234**
Scallops in Pernod Sauce **146**
Scallops with Pecorino Pesto **166**
Seafood and Saffron Soup **34**
Seafood Turnovers with Bell
　　Peppers **212**

SCAMPI

Fresh Scampi alla Parmigiana **216**
Fritto Misto di Mare **93**
Italian-Style Scampi **174**
Scampi Kebabs with Thyme and
　　Garlic **242**

SEA BASS/STRIPED BASS

Black Sea Bass with Citrus
    Marinade *228*
Mediterranean Bouillabaisse *44*
Saffron Seafood Stew *178*
Striped Bass and Chanterelles en
    Papillote *201*
Striped Bass with Coriander and
    Tomatoes *123*
Striped Bass with Tapenade and
    Artichokes *240*

SHARK

Louisiana Shark *194*

SHRIMP

Balinese Seafood Satay *232*
Chinese Fish and Seafood Stir-
    Fry *172*
Nigiri-Sushi *62*
Paella Valenciana *220*
Paprika Shrimp with Cocktail
    Sauce *102*
Saffron Seafood Stew *178*
Sautéed Shrimp with Aïoli *158*
Scallops and Shrimp on the
    Grill *234*
Seafood Gumbo *39*
Seafood Turnovers with Bell
    Peppers *212*
Shrimp and Mushroom Dim-
    Sum *107*
Shrimp, Fish and Vegetable
    Tempura *76*
Shrimp Fritters with Coriander *78*
Shrimp Salad with Garlic
    Crostini *18*
Shrimp with Caramelized
    Onions *184*
Shrimp Wonton Soup *37*
Singapore Seafood Soup with
    Coconut *52*
Singapore Shrimp *154*
Stir-Fried Shrimp with Bok-
    Choy *149*
Thai Seafood Terrines *116*

SKATE

Skate with Caper Butter *137*
Skate with Lemon and Nutmeg *185*

SNAILS

Spicy Indonesian Snail Soup with
    Papaya *47*

SOLE

Dover Sole with Shallots and
    Orange *162*

SQUID

Calamari *96*
Spicy Squid Salad, Thai Style *21*
Squid with Garlic and Black
    Peppercorns *164*
Stuffed Squid in Coriander
    Sauce *187*

SWORDFISH

Braised Swordfish with Tomato
    Sauce *189*
Fried Swordfish with Watercress *97*
Grilled Swordfish with Sun-Dried
    Tomato Sauce *246*
Sautéed Swordfish with Diced
    Vegetables *169*

TILEFISH

Seafood and Saffron Soup *34*

TROUT

Rainbow Trout with Fresh
    Herbs *105*
Salmon Trout Fillets with Asparagus
    Purée *150*
Salmon Trout Salad with Walnut Oil
    Vinaigrette *20*
Salmon Trout with Garlic
    Vinaigrette *235*
Trout Cooked in Swiss Chard
    Leaves *202*
Trout Stuffed with Pecorino Spinach
    Pesto *244*

TUNA

Fresh Tuna Carpaccio with Roasted
    Bell Peppers *65*
Maki-Sushi *60*
Nigiri-Sushi *62*
Sashimi *72*
Sicilian Tuna Pepper Steaks *239*
Tuna with Mushrooms and Herb
    Butter *152*

TURBOT

Mexican Escabèche with Orange *25*
Shrimp, Fish and Vegetable
    Tempura *76*
Turbot à la Meunière with Toasted
    Almonds *170*
Turbot Fillets in Saffron Broth *124*
Turbot, Zucchini and Eggplant
    Kebabs *248*